Will Your Vote Count?

Will Your Vote Count?
Fixing America's Broken Electoral System

HERMA PERCY, Ph.D.

PRAEGER

Westport, Connecticut
London

Library of Congress Cataloging-in-Publication Data

Percy, Herma.
 Will your vote count? : fixing America's broken electoral system / Herma Percy.
   p. cm.
 Includes bibliographical references and index.
 ISBN 978-0-313-36432-7 (alk. paper)
  1. Voting—United States. 2. Voting-machines—United States. 3. Voter registration—United States. 4. Elections—United States. I. Title.
 JK1976.P47 2009
 324.60973—dc22   2008047793

British Library Cataloguing in Publication Data is available.

Library of Congress Catalog Card Number: 2008047793
ISBN: 978-0-313-36432-7

First published in 2009

Praeger Publishers, 88 Post Road West, Westport, CT 06881
An imprint of Greenwood Publishing Group, Inc.
www.praeger.com

Printed in the United States of America

The paper used in this book complies with the
Permanent Paper Standard issued by the National
Information Standards Organization (Z39.48-1984).

10 9 8 7 6 5 4 3 2 1

In appreciation of my parents, Glen and Delma Percy, who gave me the greatest gift a parent could ever give a child for life's journey—and that is to teach me about the love of God . . . the source of my strength, courage, guidance, and peace that "pass all understanding." Thank you!

Contents

CHAPTER 3.   HOW SECURE ARE AMERICA'S VOTING
             MACHINES? CONTROVERSY AND
             MISPERCEPTIONS   29

CHAPTER 4.   VOTE DILUTION: AN ANALYSIS
             OF VOTING IRREGULARITIES   43

Tables and Figures

TABLES

FIGURES

Introduction

The one pervading evil of democracy is the tyranny of the majority, or rather of that party, not always the majority, that succeeds, by force or fraud, in carrying elections.

Lord Acton

"Voting should be simple."[1] Counting votes should be simpler. Voters in a democratic society should have confidence in this simple process that provides election results. Yet as Americans witnessed in the 2000 and 2004 presidential elections, the simple act of voting has evolved into a complicated and highly contested process. This basic right of citizenship in a democracy has become too problematic. Election mechanics and the machinery for counting the vote are rejecting an increasing number of votes rather than increasing voter participation.

The closeness of the 2000 presidential election brought to the forefront a common, yet hitherto, unnoticed phenomenon: not all votes cast for president are counted. Americans became painfully aware that their votes could be rejected due to machine malfunctions, procedural rules that varied by states, incompetent election officials, inadequate voter education, and even illegal actions. However, there is an even more important lesson that should have been learned from the 2000 presidential election crisis, a lesson that has been largely ignored by political leaders: the 2000 election fiasco was a symptom of a larger problem in our democracy. America's electoral system is broken, and the problems will increase unless we enact effective reform measures. Political scientists predict election problems will continue to occur in general elections because our electoral system was not built for high voter turnouts, close elections, high-intensity lawsuits, and voting machine technological disasters.[2]

Congress's enactment of the Help America Vote Act of 2002 (HAVA), expected to improve the mechanisms and machinery for voting, has not resolved America's election problems. HAVA mandated new election procedures and promoted the use of electronic voting machines in jurisdictions that used punch-card and lever machines. However, a new study has found that electronic voting machines may be even less reliable than the old punch cards that affected the Florida vote in the 2000 presidential election. About one-third of the nation's voters used the new voting equipment in the 2006 midterm elections; this proved to be a complicated process that affected the election results.

Current election processes and procedures are inconsistent with the principles of open and honest elections that are fundamental in a democracy. Electronic voting machines are manufactured exclusively by private companies using secret programming and source codes. The programming of electronic voting machines is done without the oversight of the federal government, which lead some computer scientists to declare insiders could program the machine to alter election results without detection. The lack of transparency and inadequate oversight of the manufacture of the voting machines undermine democratic principles and reduce voter confidence in the election process.

The problems in America's electoral system extend well beyond questionable technology. Other issues pose a threat to election integrity and democracy. A growing number of cases and complaints of voting intimidation and discrimination have marred every election since the 2000 presidential election. Furthermore, there continues to be disparate treatment in different states of provisional and absentee ballots, which dilutes the vote in many jurisdictions. An analysis of the 2004 presidential election found that at least 1.9 million voters cast provisional ballots nationwide, but in accordance with the different rules in different states, they were not all counted. The study discovered that the lack of national uniformity about which votes are counted also extends to military and overseas ballots. The disparate treatment of the provisional and absentee ballot according to where one lives, in essence, determines whether one's vote is counted or rejected, which violates the U.S. Constitution's equal protection laws.[3]

Elections are further discredited by the increasing number of election lawsuits, a trend established as a result of the 2000 election debacle: between candidates and between political parties, pitting civil rights organizations against local election officials and private citizens against voting machine manufacturers, and so on—all of which raise barriers against legitimate voters. The election process has become so chaotic that there has been an historic proliferation of activists, nonprofit organizations, academics, and ordinary citizens developing grassroots campaigns dedicated to pressure national legislators to improve the voting process. A lack of results in the U.S. Congress has led these advocates to focus as well on influencing state and local government officials to reform the broken electoral system at the local level.

Americans should be able to have confidence in election results. Our democracy and election integrity are threatened by current election standards and procedures. *Will Your Vote Count?* presents evidence that warns the nation that it is heading down the long, slippery slope to "tyranny" unless there is a restoration of political and legal boundaries to contain the effects of vote dilution and disenfranchisement.

Chapter 1

Setting the Stage: Voting Systems and the Election Crisis

Paperless [electronic] machines ensure that only the company that built them gets to count the votes, and that no one else can ever recount them.

David L. Dill, professor of computer science at Stanford University

The 2000 presidential election crisis brought to the forefront that reforms are needed in America's electoral system, particularly in election voting systems. The election fiasco highlighted the critical problems different voting machines create in our electoral system.

There are five different types of voting technologies that states use in elections: hand-counted paper ballots, mechanical lever machines, punch-cards, optical scan systems, and electronic systems. Some jurisdictions use more than one type of voting system in the same election to cast and record the vote. But how did America's electoral system evolve into these five types of voting technology, and which voting systems are the most problematic and controversial?

EVOLUTION OF VOTING SYSTEMS

Voting systems changed with developments in society or to address crippling problems in the electoral system.[1]

The hand-counted paper ballot was the first voting device used in early America.[2] Voters would receive a ballot called a prox or ticket, printed by each political party, and select a candidate or write in their own preference and place it in a ballot box. The basic ballot type developed into three forms: the Massachusetts ballot, which listed candidates by office; the Indiana ballot, which gave voters the option of choosing an entire slate or a slate with exceptions; and, later, the Australian secret ballot was implemented to reduce the corruption of vote-buying. Paper ballots are still used in some precincts. Parts of some counties in Maine, New Hampshire, Vermont, and Wisconsin use hand-counted paper ballots as one of the various types of voting technologies utilized. In recent years counties using hand-counted paper ballots "declined from 370 in 2000 to 57 in 2006."[3] Nationwide, however, the number of voters using paper ballots was reduced from 2 million (1.3 percent of voters) to 0.3 million (0.2 percent) voters from 2000–2006.[4]

The mechanical lever machine was invented around 1892, during the Industrial Revolution, to provide quicker and more reliable election results. These lever machines incorporated the casting, recording, and counting of votes into one machine. In the voting booth, voters pull a lever to select a candidate from a posted ballot. Votes are not counted manually but are recorded by advances in a counting device in the voting machine, after each vote. Election officials determine vote totals by reading the number of votes that are recorded by the counters. Some jurisdictions continue to use this older type of voting equipment. For example, all sixty-two counties in New York used lever machines in the 2006 midterm elections. In Connecticut, only about 25 of the 169 townships changed from lever machines to optical scan equipment for the 2006 midterm elections.[5]

Punch-card voting machines were adopted in 1964 as a cheaper alternative to lever machines, allowing election officials to purchase more machines and create larger precincts. The voter selects candidates by punching holes in a corresponding location on a computer card that punches out what is called a chad. The computer card, which is read and recorded by the computer, can be used for recounts. There are two types of punch-card systems: the Votomatic and the Datavote. In recent years, use of punch-card systems, which crippled many elections, has declined drastically, as will be discussed in the next section.

Optical scan voting machines, also called Marksense forms, were introduced in the 1980s to quickly compute election results. These machines had been used for decades to grade standardized examinations. Voters using the optical scan machines shade in with a pencil an oval or box, or complete an arrow that matches the name of the candidate of choice on a paper form. The computer then detects the mark and records it. In recent years, from 2000–2006, the number of counties nationwide using optical scan machines dramatically increased, from 1,279 to 1,752.[6] More than half of all voters in the United States, about 84 million, used optical scan machines in the 2006 midterm elections.[7]

Finally, the invention of computers led to the development of electronic voting machines in the 1970s. Electronic voting machines, also called direct recording electronic (DRE) machines, were similar to lever machines, but with push buttons replacing levers. Today, voters select candidates from a ballot on the computer screen by pushing a button or touching the screen. Votes are stored on a computer memory device. About 36 percent of U.S. counties used DRE machines in the 2006 midterm elections. The number of voters using electronic machines from 2000 to 2006 increased from 19.7 million to 65.9 million, the highest increase for any voting system.[8]

These five voting systems all differ in their speed, rejection rate, ballot design, recounting procedures, and capabilities. The voting technologies also differ in how each prevents and corrects errors, consequently affecting the rejection rate of each machine. In recent years, the strengths and weaknesses of each type of voting equipment have become problematic, because these variables affect whether votes are counted or rejected.

The worst and most contentious voting systems are the punch-card and electronic voting machines. There have been significant problems with their rates of accuracy and reliability in capturing the vote. These two voting systems have led to vote dilution and disenfranchisement in many jurisdictions. Florida counties' punch-card voting system severely affected the 2000 election, whereas the new electronic voting machines that replaced the punch-card system have themselves created America's new voting crisis. An assessment of these two voting systems will demonstrate how they have crippled our electoral system and pose a grave threat to our democracy.

PUNCH-CARD VOTING SYSTEM

Most Americans believed that all the votes they cast on Election Day were counted, until the 2000 presidential election brought to the forefront the high percentage of votes that were rejected on the punch-card voting system. The 2000 election debacle introduced to America a new vocabulary: *hanging chads, pregnant chads, dangling tabs, dimpled chads,* and *illegal ballots.* The punch-card system crisis highlighted the problems of the punch-card voting technology: high rejection rates, manual recount problems, poor ballot design, and inadequate machine maintenance. These problems led to numerous disputes before the courts, leading to the historic *Bush v. Gore* case and numerous other election challenges.

The 2000 Election Challenges

The complex series of the 2000 election litigations began the day after Election Day. The crisis over voting irregularities and the butterfly ballot then spread to disputes concerning legal votes in Florida, and subsequently moved to conflict over the constitutionality of Florida's election laws. Cases were litigated simultaneously in the Florida state court system and the federal court system. "There were as many as 50 separate, but often overlapping, court cases in three federal courts and five state courts."[9] Table 1.1 identifies the major cases in Florida that led to *Bush v. Gore*. Many of the extensive number of cases filed in various courts were consolidated with the major cases listed below.

Table 1.1 Timeline of the Major Cases in the 2000 Presidential Election

Cases	Date	Issue
Siegel v. LePore	Nov. 13, 2000	Constitutionality of manual recount
McDermott v. Harris	Nov. 14, 2000	Constitutionality of recount
Touchston v. McDermott	Nov. 15, 2000	Constitutionality of recount
Fla. Democratic Party v. Palm Beach Canv. Bd.	Nov. 15, 2000	Count dimpled chads
Fla. Democratic Party v. Broward County Canv. Bd.	Nov. 15, 2000	Count dimpled chads
Harris v. Circuit Judges	Nov. 15, 2000	Cease all manual recounts
Palm Beach v. Harris	Nov. 21, 2000	Certification of votes
Miami-Dade Democratic Party v. Miami Canv. Bd.	Nov. 22, 2000	Recount votes
Gore v. Miami Canv. Bd.	Nov. 23, 2000	Recount votes
Bush v. Palm Beach County Canv. Bd.	Dec. 4, 2000	Constitutionality of Florida Supreme Court's decision
Harrell v. Harris	Dec. 6, 2000	Constitutionality of manual recount
McCauley v. Bay County Canv. Bd.	Dec. 7, 2000	Absentee ballots
Bush. Hillsborough County Canv. Bd.	Dec. 8, 2000	Overseas absentee ballots
Jacobs. v. Seminole County Canv. Bd.	Dec. 8, 2000	Absentee ballots
Taylor v. Martin County Canv. Bd.	Dec. 8, 2000	Absentee ballots
Gore v. Harris	Dec. 8, 2000	Contest of the election certification
Bush v. Gore	Dec. 9, 2000	Last appeal to the U.S. Supreme Court

Source: Compiled by Percy (2003).

Evidence of a collapsing electoral system appeared not only in Florida but in other widespread election problems across the nation. Approximately eight separate lawsuits were filed—in Georgia, California, Illinois, Missouri, and Florida—on behalf of African Americans who were prevented from having their votes counted due to punch-card voting system problems. These cases and other recent cases will be discussed in Chapter 4, which examines intimidation of and discrimination against African American voters in elections, among other vote dilution issues.

Ballot Design

The ballot design of punch-card voting systems has significantly affected voters' ability to cast a ballot in recent years. In the 2000 election, the first lawsuits filed in the election debacle were from voters who challenged the constitutionality of the Palm Beach County butterfly ballot and asked for a new county-wide election.[10] Table 1.2 demonstrates the numerous cases that resulted from the poor design of the punch-card ballot. Voter confusion with the butterfly ballot attributed to the overvotes and rejection of ballots with the punch-card system in Palm Beach and Duval counties. More than 19,000 ballots were considered overvotes in Palm Beach, and 21,726 ballots in Duval County were rejected as overvotes.[11]

Spoiled Ballots

Punch-card voting systems have the highest rejection rate of ballots than any other voting system. The 2000 presidential election crisis provides a good example of this problem. There were five voting systems used in Florida's 67 counties: punch-card system in 24 counties; optical scan central tabulation in 16 counties, optical scan precinct tabulation in 25 counties; paper ballot and machine lever ballots each in only one county.[12] The *New York Times* conducted a study on rejected ballots in Florida and found about 4 percent of punch-card ballots were rejected, while only 1.4 percent of optical ballots were disqualified. The *Times* reported the following observations:

> In Orange County, the largest to use the optical equipment, only 1 in 300 ballots was blank in the presidential race. In Manatee and Brevard Counties, the rate approached 1 in 800 . . . The punch-card voting counties, by contrast . . . in Miami-Dade . . . the machines read 1 in 60 ballots as having no vote for president. In Hillsborough . . . it was 1 in 67. And in Pinellas County, it was 1 of 96.[13]

Leon County used an optical precinct tabulation system, and the spoilage rate was only 0.18 percent.[14] It had the lowest spoilage rate in the state.

Table 1.2 Butterfly-Ballot Cases in Florida in the 2000 Presidential Election

Cases	Date	Relief Sought
Horowitz v. Lepore	Nov. 9, 2000	Revote: Class action suit that ballot in Palm Beach County was illegal and violated civil rights. Relief denied.
Elkin v. LePore	Nov. 9, 2000	Revote: Ballot in Palm Beach County was illegal. Relief denied.
Gibbs v. Palm Beach County Canv. Bd.	Nov. 9, 2000	Revote: Class action suit that ballot in Palm Beach County was illegal and violated civil rights. Relief denied.
Roger v. Elections Canvassing Commission of the State of Florida	Nov. 9, 2000	Revote: Illegal Palm Beach County ballot caused voter confusion. Relief denied.
Fladell v. The Elections Canvassing Commission of the State of Florida	Nov. 9, 2000	Revote: Illegal Palm Beach County ballot caused voter confusion. Relief denied.
Lichtman v. Bush	Nov. 14, 2000	Misconduct by Palm Beach County Supervisor of election for selecting confusing butterfly ballot for the election. Relief denied.
HABIL v. Palm Beach County Can. Bd.	Nov. 14, 2000	Revote: Voting irregularities that included poll workers voting for Haitians, and language assistance being denied. Relief denied.
Katz v. Florida Elections Canvassing Commission of the State of Florida	Nov. 17, 2000	New Election: Ballot in Palm Beach was illegal. Relief denied.
Brown v. Stafford	Dec. 5, 2000	Duvall County ballot was illegal and violated civil rights. Relief denied.

Source: Compiled by Percy (2003).

The U.S. Commission on Civil Rights conducted a public hearing and took testimonies from election officials that tried to explain the reasons for the disparities. Ion Sancho, who served as supervisor of elections for 12 years in Florida's Leon County, testified, "I can see somewhere in the neighborhood of 90,000 people, in my opinion, were disenfranchised in the punchcard jurisdictions."[15] He blamed the problems on the lack of voter education by the state and failure to train its workers. He also stated, "Florida as a state spent not one dollar on radio and TV ads informing voters how to vote. This in a state that in the past has spent over $35 million in one year telling Floridians how to play the lottery."[16]

Counties that used precinct-based optical counting system (PBC) had a far lower rejection ballot rate. The PBC system detects overvotes, and the voter is given another chance to correct the ballot. Voters who cast their ballots in precincts that did not use the PBC had their votes counted at an offsite location, and their votes were lost at a rate of five times higher than citizens who voted in counties that used the counting technology.[17]

> On average, the spoilage rate for counties using the precinct-based optical scan technology was 0.83 percent, far lower than the average spoilage rates for either central-based optical scan technology (5.68 percent) or central based punch-card technology (3.93 percent) . . . 22 of the 23 counties with the lowest spoilage rates used precincts-based optical scan technology.[18]

The high ballot-rejection rate of the punch-card system may have been attributed, in part, to maintenance of the voter system. Jim Smith, co-chairperson of the Governor's Select Task Force on Election Procedures, Standards and Technology, observed that "some of the voting machines are more than 30 years old. I mean some of them hadn't been clean in years . . . what they found out in Dade County, one reason they had a significant problem with chads is the machines hadn't been cleaned, maybe ever."[19] Florida's Governor Select Task Force on Election Procedures, Standards, and Technology studied election reform after the 2000 election and acknowledged, "In statewide or national elections, when different kinds of voting systems with different error rates are used, every voter does not have the same chance to have his or her vote counted accurately."[20] The various problems of the punch-card voting system drastically denied voters of their right to vote and affected election results.

Florida Legislature

The punch-card voting crisis in the 2000 election was multifaceted in complications. A significant area of the election crisis, that is rarely discussed, was the proceedings of the Florida Legislature that created the Select Joint Committee on the Manner of Appointment of Presidential Electors to determine its legal authority to select electors for the office of the President.[21] It was an unprecedented act by a state that resulted from the crisis of punch-card voting system. The legislature feared the election contest that challenged the problems of the punch-card system, and Florida's election laws would not be resolved by the national deadline for Congress to receive and count the votes of Florida's certified electors. In a series of hearings by the Joint Committee, testimony was given by numerous election law experts, law professors, constitutional scholars, and the general public advising the legislature on whether it should intervene in the election process and select its own slate of electors.

The Joint Committee, in an 8–5 vote, recommended that the legislature convene in a special session to take action to ensure that Florida's 25 electoral votes were counted.[22] The Florida Legislature was prepared to submit its own slate of electors to meet—what it considered—its constitutional obligation. It was a peculiar and troubling decision, which resulted from the punch-card voting crisis. It was halted, fortunately, by the Supreme Court's decision in *Bush v. Gore*. The verdict ended the 2000 election crisis of the punch-card machines, and many jurisdictions have since replaced them with electronic voting machines.

ELECTRONIC VOTING SYSTEM

After the 2000 election debacle, Congress enacted the Help America Vote Act (HAVA) to replace punch-card voting systems and upgrade voting technology nationwide. The 2002 Act granted $3.8 billion to states to improve their voting process by the 2006 midterm elections. Thus, the replacement of the punch-card voting machines with the new electronic voting machines became widespread and has sharply increased in recent years.

Growth in the Use of Electronic Machines

In the 1980s, only two states used electronic voting machines, California and Illinois—in only seven counties combined.[23] In the 2004 general election, approximately 50 million registered voters, in about 675 counties, used electronic voting machines, accounting for around 30 percent of all registered voters. In the 2006 midterm elections about 38.4 percent of voters or 65.9 million voters used direct recording voting equipment. Only thirteen Idaho counties used the punch-card system in the 2006 midterm election, since the 2000 punch-card disaster in Florida.[24]

The use of direct recording machines increased in the 2008 elections as DREs are also used to read optical scan ballots. Table 1.3 illustrates the voting equipment changes since the 2000 election and indicates the sharp increase in electronic equipment.

Although the use of electronic machines has become widespread, there are several complications and controversies surrounding these machines. After the 2000 election crisis, manufacturers of electronic machines promoted them as the solution to voting problems. They also lobbied states to purchase their voting systems. Additionally, Congress provided incentives to the states to overhaul their voting systems via HAVA, which led to the rapid adoption of electronic voting machines. This rush to replace old punch-card and lever machines neglected a comprehensive and measured

Table 1.3 Voting Equipment Changes by Equipment Type,
2000–2006—Counties

Type of Voting Equipment	Number of Counties			
	Nov–2000	Nov–2002	Nov–2004	Nov–2006
Punch cards	572	459	330	13
Lever machines	434	288	264	62
Hand-counted paper ballots	370	304	298	57
Optically scanned paper ballots	1,279	1,360	1,443	1,752
Electronic (DRE) equipment	309	547	631	1,142
Mixed (multiple types)	149	156	148	92
TOTAL	3,113	3,114	3,114	3,118

Source: Election Data Services, "2006 Voting Equipment Study," October 2, 2006, p. 4.

assessment of electronic voting machines. There are various security and reliability problems with electronic machines. In addition, there are many divisive issues about the manufacturers of electronic voting machines that center on conflict of interest, oversight, and ownership.

Manufacturers of Electronic Voting Systems

The major manufacturers of electronic voting systems have been strongly criticized because it is believed the machines are susceptible to manipulation and error. There are a growing number of activists who challenge the manufacturers of electronic voting machines. There are five major manufacturers of electronic machines: Diebold Election Systems manufactures AccuVote-TS; Sequoia Voting System manufactures AVC Advantage; Microvote Corporation manufactures Microvote DRE and MV-464; Election Systems and Software (ES&S) manufactures Votronic and iVotronic; and different vendors manufacture Shouptronic 1242 DRE. Election Systems & Software, Diebold, and Sequoia manufacture at least 80 percent of the voting equipment in the nation.[25] According to one critic of the industry, there are also various defense contractors that also provide election services including Accenture (a business partner of Halliburton), National Semiconductor Corporation, Northrop Grumman/Diversified Dynamics/TRW (partners with Science Applications International Corporation), Hart Intercivic, General Dynamics/Computing Devices Canada, Perot Systems

Government Services, Inc., Unisys (partners with ES&S), and Booz-Allen & Hamilton.[26]

Election activists cite several areas of concern about the ownership of electronic voting machines. There is growing uneasiness that a significant amount of voting machines is owned by foreign corporations. For example, Accenture, based in Bermuda was the contractor to develop Election .com, the online military vote in 2004.[27] "Election.com was formerly owned by Osan, Ltd., a Saudi Arabian firm."[28] Sequoia Voting System is a British-based company, EVS is affiliated with Japan, and N.V. Nederlandsche Apparantenfrariek is affiliated with Netherlands.[29] There are also several companies worldwide that are involved in some aspect of the manufacture of electronic voting machines.

The manufacturers of electronic voting machines have also been criticized for the overlapping of ownership in the industry and conflict of interest. "Many voting machine companies appear to share managers, investors, and equipment which raises questions of . . . monopolistic practices."[30] In addition, two major manufacturers that count a large percentage of votes nationwide are owned by brothers.

> The voting machine company Datamark, which became American Information Systems and is known as ES&S, was founded in 1980 by two brothers, Bob and Todd Urosevich. Today, Todd is a vice president at ES&S and Bob is CEO of Diebold Elections Systems.[31]

Critics also contend there is inadequate oversight of the manufacturers of voting machines. The federal government has limited regulatory authority of the companies. It does not oversee the manufacture and programming of the voting machines. In addition, one election activist stated, "there are no government standards or restrictions on who can sell and service voting machines and systems. Foreigners, convicted criminals, office holders, political candidates, and news media organizations can and do own these companies."[32] Moreover, critics assert that some standards of the federal certification of voting equipment are outdated and voluntary guidelines, not mandatory specifications.

It is important to note that although strong accusations have been levied against the manufacturers of electronic voting machines, this investigation found no substantiated reports of impropriety in any election by these manufacturers.

Voting systems are increasingly becoming obstacles for voters in every election. Eight years after the 2000 election crisis signaled the need for America to reform its voting system the election process still remains problematic. Electronic voting technology that replaced faulty punch-card machines has created more voting problems in elections, and consequently a new crisis that needs to be addressed by political leaders.

Chapter 2

Reliability: Voting Machine Problems

> I'm not going to put this paper on my machines—it'll be over my dead body, because I just don't think it works.
>
> Linda Lamone, Maryland State Elections Administrator

More than 80 percent of the nation's voters cast some type of electronic ballot in the 2008 presidential election. In recent years, electronic voting systems have come under fire as machine malfunctions have compromised elections in about half the states. Reports of votes "being subtracted, swapped and deleted during elections" have marred the voting process.[1] These new computerized voting machines have left voters with serious concerns about election results. There are still many unanswered questions concerning the reliability of these machines such as: What if electronic voting machines fail at thousands of polling sites? What if electronic machines switch people's votes or lose their votes? What if there is a power failure during an election conducted on electronic voting machines—will the voting still be possible? What if the margin of victory was close in a presidential election and there was no way to recount the results?[2]

The unreliability of voting machines rose to national attention in the 2000 election debacle. Voting machine malfunctions have since persisted and increased in every election. In the 2008 presidential primaries there were voting machine malfunctions and disputed results. In the 2006 midterm elections, there were five times more voter complaints to election hotlines than in the 2004 general election; about 16.9 percent of complaints concerned mechanical problems.[3] Mechanical problems nationwide in recent elections include voting machines that would not start or scan ballots, votes cast for the wrong candidate, failure to operate correctly, and failure to count ballots as cast. Additional voting machine problems include confusing voting screens, machines that are inaccessible to disabled voters, "machines undelivered to the polls, poll workers that cannot operate the machines," and long lines due to malfunctioning or few machines.[4] These voting problems, as a result of unreliable voting machines, create obstacles to voters and significantly affect election results.

ASSESSMENT OF MACHINE MALFUNCTIONS, BY STATE

All elections in this decade have been riddled with voting machine problems. There are many horrifying examples in about half the states that indicate voting machines did not accurately count the vote and affected election results. Electronic voting machines proved unreliable in states such as Alabama, Arizona, California, Colorado, Florida, Georgia, Illinois, Indiana, Kansas, Louisiana, Maryland, Michigan, Minnesota, Missouri, New Jersey, New Mexico, North Carolina, Ohio, Pennsylvania, South Carolina, Texas, Utah, Virginia, and Wisconsin. An assessment of machine malfunctions in these states in the 2008 presidential primaries, the 2004 presidential election, and the 2002 and 2006 midterm elections will show these electronic voting systems pose a threat to our American system of democracy.

Alabama

In the 2002 race for governor in Alabama, the malfunction of the electronic voting machine, Election System & Software (ES&S), critically affected the outcome of the election. In Baldwin County, approximately 6,300 votes were lost, and there were reports that votes flipped from the Democrat candidate to the Republican candidate.

The Democrat candidate, Don Siegelman, requested a recount but it was denied and led to his defeat to Republican Bob Riley. Mark Kelly of ES&S responded to the mysterious vote loss that cost Siegelman the election by stating, "Something happened. I don't have enough intelligence to say exactly what."[5] The clear malfunction of the electronic voting machines compromised the governor's election in Alabama.

Arizona

There have been various problems in recent presidential elections in Arizona. In the 2008 presidential primary, there were various reports of irregularities as voters' names were missing from the registration rolls, and polling locations changed without voter notification. There were also identifications problems at polling sites and voters were not given provisional ballots.[6]

Election problems also occurred in the 2004 presidential election. There were numerous voting machines that rejected many ballots. There were several incidents in which machines failed to read the ballots or broke down. Voting problems have been increasing in elections in the state and are significantly affecting the outcome of elections.

California

In the hotly contested 2008 presidential primary, the state encountered various election problems. Voting machines were disabled, and some were not delivered to several polling locations. In one of the most populous jurisdictions, Los Angeles, the ink for seven booths at one polling station was not delivered. Voters were sent to other polling places to vote, although it was inconvenient for some and unfeasible for others. In Santa Clara County, about five precincts ran out of ballots. In Alameda County, more than a dozen precincts did not have enough ballots.[7] In Beverly Hills there were voting machine malfunctions and an insufficient amount of poll workers to work in the precincts.

> "Four of California's most populous counties—Riverside, San Bernardino, San Diego and Santa Clara—count[ed] votes at centralized locations because there [weren't] enough optical scanners for every precinct. Los Angeles and Sacramento also haul[ed] their paper ballots to a single location, where they [were] tallied electronically."[8]

California was ordered by the court in a lawsuit following the 2000 election to replace faulty punch-card voting machines before the 2004 presidential election.[9] California then changed its use of punch-card machines to electronic voting machines. But these machines proved to be unreliable in capturing the vote in the 2006 midterm elections. There were reports that electronic voting machines crashed in the state. In addition, polling sites opened late while poll workers struggled to operate voting machines in Kern County and other counties. After these tumultuous voting problems the state worked to replace its electronic voting machines for the 2008 presidential election. As a result, in the 2008 presidential primary, the state used paper ballots, but there were still election problems. Petitions circulated in the state disputing the voting process in the 2008 presidential primary.

Colorado

Several voting machine problems were reported in Colorado in the 2004 presidential election. Several counties in Colorado that used some form of electronic voting machine experienced problems, including optical scanner machines that did not work. An election monitor for the Elections Protection Coalition in Larimer County reported, "Computers were down and approximately 150 voters were turned away and told to go to other polling places."[10] It is important to note that paper ballots were not given to voters or provisional ballots at the time the problems were reported.

In the 2004 election, malfunctioning machines were also left in service for voters to use, even when poll workers knew the machines were not working properly. In Arapahoe County, a voter reported that the machine malfunctioned when he tried to cast his ballot and the "poll worker tended to the machine in a way that zeroed out the vote. The official said the machine had been acting up all day, but that it was still in service because they only had two machines."[11] The voter reported that, though he was given a provisional ballot to cast a ballot, he noticed the machine was still left in service.

In Denver, voters at one crowded polling place could not vote because the precinct ran out of provisional ballots. Voters complained that some had waited as much as two hours, and the ballots still had not appeared. A nonpartisan voting education group, Fair Vote Colorado, reported there were shortages of ballots at other sites in Denver. These voting problems in the state have lowered voter confidence in the election process.

Florida

The problems with Florida's voting machines in the 2000 presidential election have been well documented in this book. Unfortunately, the voting machine problems did not end with the 2000 election crisis. Many counties replaced the punch-card system with electronic voting systems, but similar problems occurred again in the 2004 election. In Palm Beach, Miami-Dade, Broward, and Pinellas counties, there were disabled electronic voting machines, or machines that did not accurately record votes for the president. "In Florida's Broward County, home to Fort Lauderdale, some [machine] tallies were counting backward. After reaching 32,000 the maximum number of votes that [this] particular software program could handle, the machine started subtracting votes instead of adding them."[12] Optical scanners were also not working properly in Brevard and Leon counties.[13] Also in "a house seat in Florida, paperless voting terminals record[ed] 134 cast ballots as blank. The race ended up being decided by a margin of twelve votes. Left without printed record, election officials could not recapture how voters intended to chose and the results stood."[14] In Deerfield Beach, in a predominantly African American community, some voting machines did not work, and no paper ballots were given to voters. The precinct also did not open for about two hours.

Voting problems also persisted in midterm elections throughout the state. In 2006, in a close race in Sarasota County, about 17,000 ballots were cast on the iVotronic touch-screen voting machines. In this close race there was a 369-vote difference between the candidates, and the electronic voting machines could not perform a recount as Florida law permits in close races.[15] In other problematic races in Florida, some poll workers could not operate the machines in the 2002 mid-term elections in Miami, which led to a large number of voters being unable to vote. The inspector general could not audit the results in those races. In a 2002 runoff election in Wellington, Florida, about seventy-eight votes were not recorded by voting machines for the only race on the ballot. The precincts used the electronic voting machine, ES&S. It was a close race, plagued with machine malfunction, which was decided by only five votes.[16] Electronic voting machines also failed voters in a number of other counties in Florida.

Georgia

Recent elections in Georgia have been entangled with voting problems that have led to disputes before the courts. The most recent voting problem in the state occurred in the 2008 presidential primary. There were voting machine malfunctions in Fulton County. This county also experienced machine mishaps in the 2002 and 2006 midterm elections. In the 2002 midterm elections there were questionable voting procedures in Fulton County in which the "memory cards (ballot box) of sixty-seven electronic voting machines had been misplaced so ballots cast on those machines were left out of previously announced vote totals. Fifty-six cards, containing 2,180 ballots were located, but eleven memory cards still were missing two days after the election."[17] Other counties that had missing memory cards included Bibb County, Glynn County, and Dekalb County.[18] There were also other machine malfunctions in the 2006 midterm elections that led to problems in Dekalb County. The voting problems in these and other counties prevented many citizens from voting.

Illinois

Every election in Illinois in this decade has been problematic. In the 2008 presidential primary at least nine precincts in Chicago had significant voting machine problems. Additionally, about twenty voters in the city's North Side were given a stylus for marking the electronic touch-screens that did not record votes. The voters complained that the equipment did not mark their choices on the paper ballot, and the precinct worker told the voters it was "invisible ink" that was used to mark the ballots. These ballots were rejected, and only about ten of those voters were able to vote again. The other ten citizens were disenfranchised. On the West side of the city voting discrepancies led to poll workers getting into a fist fight, and police were called to the scene and took one election judge into custody.[19] There were missing voting machines and ballots from some polling sites. Electronic voting machines were reported as being very slow, which prolonged the amount of time voters had to wait in line to vote.

Voting problems also occurred in other elections in the state. In the 2006 midterm elections, the voting rights organization, People for the American Way, recruited about three thousand election judges with computer experience to help monitor voting machines on Election Day 2006. They found that many poll workers did not receive adequate hands-on training to operate the electronic machines. The *USA Today* also reported in 2006 that there were voting machine paper misfeeds, missing memory cartridges for electronic machines containing election results, and extensive delays in counting ballots.[20]

Similarly in the 2004 presidential election, voting machines malfunctioned in various ways in the state. Some machines failed to function, while others cast overvotes or undervotes. In several of these cases, voters reported that even when the voting machine indicated an "undervote," the vote was still cast; meaning voters were only able to cast incomplete votes. In Cook County, there were numerous reports of poll workers that could not operate the voting machines and machines that failed to operate. Other problems in 2004 that occurred with the electronic machines included voter cards getting stuck in the machines or the machines froze up. These voting problems in recent elections all created obstacles to the free exercise to vote.

Indiana

In the 2004 presidential election there were major problems at the polls. It was reported that voting machines in more than half the precincts in Indianapolis and Marion County could not start. The *Indianapolis Star* reported that as a result of poll workers' inability to operate the machines about one hundred and seventy-five precincts had to use paper ballots. In Delaware County, the cards to activate the machines were not correctly programmed in seventy-five precincts. Machine problems reduced the poll hours for voters, but a court extended the voting time to allow voters sufficient time to vote. In Marion County, there were various problems with touch-screen machines that were not working in more than 10 percent of the county's precincts. There was also the problem of voting machines recording more votes than voters at the polls. "An Indiana county listed each of its precincts as having 300 votes for a total of 22,220 when in reality there's a total of 79,000."[21] Similar problems occurred in a November 2003 off-year election in Boone County. The MicroVote voting machines counted 144,000 votes when only 5,352 existed. Micro Vote fixed the malfunction, but County officials were troubled by the occurrence of the problem.[22] These recent voting problems in the state have led to disputes before the courts.

Kansas

In recent midterm elections in Kansas there have been reports of election voting problems. In Johnson County, poll workers in the 2006 midterm elections had to find creative solutions to keep the voting cards from splitting. The Election Protection Coalition,[23] comprising numerous voting and civil rights organizations, reported the following:

> Enterprising poll workers in Kansas are using hand lotion to solve sporadic problems with the county's touch-screen voting system. Machines have rejected the encoded cards that voters plug into the machines, forcing shutdowns and re-coding.[24]

Voting machine problems also occurred in the 2002 midterm elections. In Clay County in the 2002 commissioner primaries, malfunctioned voting machines showed candidate Jerry Mayo receiving 48 percent of the votes and therefore lost the race. But a hand recount of the votes by election officials revealed that Mayo actually won by a landslide with 76 percent of the vote.[25] These miscounts by electronic machines created confusion in the election process.

Louisiana

There were many voting machine problems in the 2004 presidential election and the 2002 midterm elections. At some polling sites all the voting machines broke down at their locations on Election Day. At other polling places there were insufficient voting machines for voters, which created long lines and frustrated some voters. "In one polling place in Orleans County, all three machines were down from 6 A.M. to 9 A.M. [Voters] reported that at least forty-nine people were unable to vote."[26] Many voters left the polling site without voting in the election.

Similarly, in the 2002 election, disabled voting machines in Ascension Parish affected voting in many precincts. "An elections official gnashed his teeth as more than two hundred machine malfunctions were called in. The Parish Clerk said his staff was on the road repairing machines from 5 A.M. to 9 P.M. In one case, a machine was not repaired until 12:30 A.M. Wednesday."[27] These machine problems disenfranchised many voters who were unable to vote.

Maryland and Virginia

The switch to electronic voting machines in the state of Maryland created voting problems in the 2006 midterm elections. "There were about 300–500 people waiting 2–3 hours to vote at a location in Prince George's county because several machines are down."[28] There were few computer technicians to assist with the voting machine problems. There were also fewer poll workers to work at the polling sites who were sufficiently trained to operate the machines, such as the elderly. Voters had problems selecting the candidate of choice using the electronic voting machines. A voter in Baltimore reported that when he tried to vote for the candidate for governor, O'Malley, the other candidate's name, Ehrlich, kept appearing on the screen. He said his wife also reported the same thing happened when she tried to vote. Similarly, the Election Protection Coalition reported that one voter said the "ballot for candidates only stayed up for a few seconds, and he wasn't able to vote for a candidate. All of the other voting questions stayed up for ample time."[29] The voter cards that are used with electronic voting machines also created significant problems. One voter in Baltimore stated she "was 21st in line at the 7 A.M. opening. Everyone was given his or her electronic cards. When [they] tried to vote, all machines went down but [the] card was already processed. She was sent back and forth between the "machine" judges and the "cards" judges. Finally she just voted by provisional ballot."[30] Another voter in Baltimore claimed when she tried to insert her voting card in the voting machines it indicated, "She had already voted. Then [she was] told to vote provisionally. Then they had her vote on another electronic machine on some random card."[31]

Neighboring state Virginia also reported similar problems with the new electronic voting machines in the 2006 midterm election. "In Virginia (and other states), officials were not able to report results from electronic voting systems until well after polls closed because of DRE problems. In the Virginia elections, voters in one county noted that their votes were change[d] as they voted on DREs."[32] The voting problems that occurred in the 2006 elections led Maryland, after the election, to conduct a study about electronic voting machines. This study, which is discussed in the next chapter, indicated electronic voting machines were unreliable and insecure. The research findings led to lawsuits in the state to mandate voter-verified paper trails for electronic machines to better ensure the integrity of elections. The state adopted the voter-verified paper trail system and used the electronic voting machines in the 2008 presidential election.

Michigan

There were numerous election problems in the 2004 presidential election in Michigan. Voting machines did not work at some precincts, and some polling places opened late in the struggle to get the machines to work. Voters were confused at many precincts on how to use the voting machines, and inadequately trained poll workers could not provide assistance. In Warren County, "a first time voter was denied the opportunity to vote. He had difficulty with the lever used to close the booth and when he asked a question, he was told to use the lever to close it. However, closing it caused him to cast a blank ballot. Then he was told to leave because there were no provisions for his mistakes."[33] Another problem was that some ballots were improperly handled or not counted at all.[34]

In Oakland County, voters complained of jammed voting machine scanners that left many voters unsure if their votes would be counted. Poll workers instructed some voters to place their ballots in a "bin" with ballots already scanned. The poll workers told the voters they could wait for the repairman, but voters left after waiting for almost an hour and a half. In Wayne County, there were faulty ballot scanners on electronic voting machines. At one location the scantron tabulator on the voting machine was broken for two hours, and a voter reported that "voters were getting ballots and voting but votes were not being counted on site. A poll worker stated they would count the votes later."[35] The Election Protection (EP) Coalition volunteers that were sent to monitor the 2004 election noted that at one polling place in Genesee County "when the optical scan receptacle for taking the ballots jammed, the election judge came to the front of the building and announced 'polls closed.' The EP volunteer called city clerk's office, but no additional help was available."[36] The combination of jammed voting machines, broken scanners, and closed polls diluted the vote in the 2004 election.

Minnesota

Voting machines with scanning problems occurred in recent Minnesota elections. In the 2004 presidential election, voters contacted the election protection hotline to complain that scanning machines of electronic voting systems were broken and prevented them from voting.

Some voters complained the counters on the voting machines did not move or advance when a new vote was cast. Voters were concerned if their votes would count in the presidential election if the ballots were not properly scanned. In addition, poll workers at one polling site in Hennepin told a language translator that she could not assist voters. An attorney with the EP Coalition who was present to monitor the elections "intervened," which allowed the translator to assist voters who requested assistance.[37]

Missouri

St. Louis experienced voting problems in the recent 2008 presidential primary election. Power lines at two polling stations were knocked out by the strong winds and a storm on Election Day in St. Louis County. Some voters left the precinct unable to cast a ballot.

There were several problems at polling sites in St. Louis. At some polling locations the box that contained all the voting materials was jammed. Poll workers at another polling site had difficulty obtaining election materials that were locked in a closet at the precinct. In the Logo Elementary precinct, it was also reported that some poll workers and voters did not know how to use the voting machines properly. As a result, poll workers reported that voters cast their paper ballots incorrectly into the voting machines. Also, about thirty election judges were late and alternate individuals had to replace them at polling sites across the city. There were also lengthy delays with poll openings, of almost two hours, at some polling stations and some voters left being unable to vote. Similarly, in the 2004 presidential election, voters in St. Charles, St. Louis, Ray, and Jackson counties were confused on how to properly cast their vote using the punch-card ballots. They filed complaints with the EP volunteers. There are also reports of polling places opening late and closing early.[38]

New Jersey

In the 2008 presidential primary, electronic voting machines failed to operate at some polling places. Some voters left without being able to cast a ballot. Even the New Jersey Governor Jon Corzine had to wait for about an hour to vote when the voting machines failed to work at his precinct, the Hoboken Fire Department Engine Company No. 2.[39] As a result of the voting problems in the primary, activists asked the court to determine whether electronic voting machines in New Jersey are reliable.[40] A New Jersey judge granted computer scientists the authority to examine the Sequoia touch-screen voting machines used in the primary that malfunctioned and did not accurately record votes in about six counties in the 2008 presidential primary.

New Jersey also experienced voting machine problems with the Sequoia voting machines in the 2000 presidential election. A Sequoia voting machine was removed from the polling place in Middlesex County after sixty-five ballots were cast and no votes were recorded. In the 2002 midterm elections about forty-six machines malfunctioned and prevented voters from casting a ballot. It was reported that "about 96 percent of the voting machines couldn't register votes for mayor, despite the machines having been pre-tested and certified for use."[41] New Jersey was ordered to switch to paper-based voting system by January 1, 2008, but the deadline was extended to June 2008.

New Mexico

Election problems have been on the increase in New Mexico. In the 2008 presidential primary more than six polling sites ran out of ballots. There have been reports of malfunctioning machines, and voters are concerned about whether their votes are counted. As a result of the unreliable electronic voting machines Governor Bill Richardson said the state would replace the machines with optical scanners that count paper ballots. In the 2004 presidential election in Bernalillo County, a voter that used an electronic voting machine reported to EP that "after selecting a Democratic candidate, [he] noticed that the Republican light actually lit up. He had to select the Democratic candidate again to cancel it out, and then select it again to make the correct selection. He had to do this for almost all the people he voted for."[42]

An EP volunteer that was assigned to monitor the precinct also reported a similar occurrence. He stated that while helping an elderly voter he "witnessed that when the Democrat Presidential candidate was selected, the Libertarian candidate would be highlighted."[43] Similar irregularities with touch-screen machines were reported in other area precincts during the 2004 early voting in the state.

North Carolina

There have been various computer glitches and procedural problems that affected whether votes were counted in the 2004 presidential election and the 2002 midterm election. North Carolina experienced the most serious malfunction of e-voting systems in the 2004 presidential election. The state used the UniLect Corporation e-voting system and lost over 4,500 ballots in the voting system. It was also reported that some votes were lost because the computer could not hold "as much data as officials originally thought."[44]

Several election problems also occurred in jurisdictions such as Carteret County. Voting problems included machines that jammed, torn ballots, vote counters that did not advance after additional votes were scanned, and problems with optical scan machines. Additionally, ballot receipts given to voters indicated that the votes were not recorded, but poll workers told voters not be concerned about it.[45] The following was also reported in Carteret County:

> The touch-screen machines lost more than four thousand votes in Carteret County because of programming errors, leaving one statewide race in limbo as the margin of victory for one candidate fell far short of the missing votes. That led to a recent decision by the county board of elections to get rid of the machines, creating what could be a scramble to find a new system in time.[46]

Similar voting problems occurred in the 2002 midterm elections. "In North Carolina . . . six touch-screen machines malfunctioned and deleted

436 electronic ballots. In a post election investigation, the manufacturer determined that the machines erroneously had stopped counting votes even while the polls were still open."[47] In some counties there were problems in vote tabulation. In Wayne County, voting machines skipped several thousand votes for candidates of both parties. An evaluation of the voting machines found additional votes for candidates and in some cases reversed the elections.[48] Also in 2002 in Wake County, "one out of four new touchscreen voting machines failed in early voting, losing 294 votes. Election workers looked for the 294 voters to ask them to vote again."[49] These and other machine malfunctions affected many recent elections in the state.

Ohio

In the 2008 democratic presidential primary, both candidates reported receiving "troubling reports of irregularities." One poll worker was removed from a precinct in Akron for "aggressively challenging voters."[50] Election problems in Ohio have been increasing in recent years. The 2004 presidential election in Ohio had more problems than any other state. There were voting problems all around the state, from disabled voting machines, to incorrect vote tallies, and polling sites with few voting machines. This led to long lines, and some voters left unable to vote. In Mahoning County there were incidents of "flipped votes." The *Washington Post* reported that twenty-five electronic machines in Youngstown flipped votes from John Kerry to President Bush. The case *Moss v. Bush* also noted that voting machines in one precinct in Youngstown strangely recorded a negative twenty-five million votes.[51] The EP Coalition received numerous complaints from voters, and one voter in Mahoning County said, "Every time I tried to vote for the Democratic Party Presidential [candidate] the machine went blank. I had to keep trying, it took five tries."[52] In some precincts in Mahoning County voting machines counted more votes than voters.

> For example, in CMP 4C Precinct, there were 279 signatures and 280 machine votes. In BLV 1 Precinct, there were 396 signatures, but 398 machine votes. In AUS 12 Precinct, there were 372 signatures, but 376 machine votes. In POT 1 Precinct, there were 479 signatures, but 482 machine votes, and in YGN 6F Precinct, there were 270 signatures, but 273 machine votes.[53]

Similar election problems occurred in Cuyahoga County. "In Cuyahoga County, where Cleveland is located, there appeared to be more votes cast than the number of registered voters in the region."[54] In Gahanna County, a suburb of Columbus, electronic machines "gave Bush 4,258 votes to

Kerry's 260. But the precinct has only 800 votes, and only 365 of them voted Republican. Votes were recorded onto a malfunctioning cartridge."[55]

Voting machines have been problematic, not only for voters, but also for poll workers who were charged with instructing voters. Confused poll workers gave incorrect information to voters in Cuyahoga County, which led to a large number of votes for a third-party candidate in the 2004 election. "Ballots were fed into the wrong machine, switching Kerry votes into third party votes. This was done on the advice of poll workers who told voters that they could insert their ballots into any open machines and machines were not clearly marked indicating that they would work only for their designated precinct."[56] The ballot design for the voting machines used in Cuyahoga County also confused voters and poll workers.

There were other kinds of machine malfunctions in Cuyahoga County in the 2004 presidential election. There were machines that flipped votes, and voters had to vote on machines that election officials knew were disabled. One voter complained to EP Coalition when she tried to correct the problem she was "told by election officials that the machine had been having problems all morning."[57] A voter reported "Every time I tried to vote for the Democratic Party Presidential [candidate], the machine went blank. I had to keep trying, it took five tries."[58] One polling place closed at 9:25 A.M. on Election Day because none of the voting machines would work.

Another 2004 election problem in Ohio was the use of punch-card voting machines that resulted in spoiled ballots, similar to the Florida 2000 election. "In Cleveland zip codes where at least 85 percent of the population is black, precinct results show that one in thirty-one ballots registered no vote for president, more than twice the rate of largely white zip codes where one in seventy-five registered no vote for president. Election officials say that nearly 77,000 of the 96,000 spoiled ballots were punch cards."[59] The U.S. House of Representative Judiciary Committee investigated Ohio's 2004 presidential election and found voting problems in many counties including discrepancies in vote totals in Perry and Trumbull counties. For example, in Perry County the committee found the following:

> In W Lexington G AB, 350 voters are registered according to the County's initial tallies. Yet, 434 voters cast ballots. As the tallies indicate this would be an impossible 124 percent voter turnout. The breakdown on election night was initially reported to be 174 votes for Bush and 246 votes for Kerry. We are advised that Perry County Board of Elections has since issued a correction, claiming that due to a computer error, some votes were counted twice.[60]

Similar overvotes occurred in other places in Perry County such as Madison and Monroe townships. The EP Coalition testified to the House Judiciary

Committee that more than 3,300 incidents of voting irregularities occurred in Ohio in the 2004 presidential election.[61]

In Franklin County there were reports that voting machines were undelivered to many precincts with a large African American voter population.

> There were 102,000 newly registered voters, many of whom were African American, either 81 or 125 voting machines were never deployed to precincts. As a result, some voters in inner city Columbus— mostly African American Democrats—had to wait in line up to seven hours to cast their ballot, while an unknown number gave up and went home.[62]

In Franklin and Hamilton counties there were also reports of voting machine glitches and procedural problems that affected vote totals. In Franklin County, the following was reported:

> Three of five machines down, and voters stood in line from 6:30 A.M. to 11:30 A.M. before voting. [In Hamilton], voter[s] attempted to vote YES on issue 4 and NO on issue 5, but the machine wouldn't allow the vote on issue 5. Ballot only accepted the vote on issue 5 when issue 4 was left blank.[63]

Voting problems also occurred in the 2006 midterm elections. The EP Coalition reported that in Cleveland "some of the machines were not working, some machines were having paper malfunction and they would just quit in the middle of the voting. People (were) not sure that their votes went through."[64] In Cuyahoga County about 143 machines broke down. Many precincts had printers that jammed or powered down. "More than two hundred encoders that create cards for voters to vote were missing. The machines produced errors at high rates. One audit of the election discovered that in 72.5 percent of the audited machines, the paper trial did not match the digital tally on the memory cards."[65] These varied voting problems tainted the 2004 and 2006 election in Ohio and led to several lawsuits to reform election procedures in the state.

Pennsylvania

There have been numerous reports from voters throughout Pennsylvania about voting problems in recent elections. In the 2006 midterm elections there were several complaints about voting problems from voters, volunteers, and election officials to EP in counties such as Philadelphia, Allegheny, Montgomery, Delaware, Berks, Lehigh, and Dauphin.

In the 2006 midterm elections, *The Daily News* reported that more than one hundred voting machines were broken when the polls opened on

Election Day. In Allegheny County, machines did not work and there were no paper or provisional ballots for voters in many locations. There were reports that voting machine problems delayed voting in counties such as Philadelphia and Lebanon, which also had insufficient ballots for voters. In Wilkes-Barre, volunteers for election monitoring groups reported there were countywide voting machines that were out of synch. "The machines zeroed out in the morning and the time calibrated. By the end of the day, they were an hour off and they were shutting down an hour prior to the polls closing. The machines had to be manually reset and there is a question of whether the votes are actually counted once the machines were reset."[66] In Delaware County, voting machines prevented voters from casting a ballot for candidates from different parties. The machine would only allow voters to vote a straight party ticket. Malfunctioning voting machines severely affected the elections in the state.

In the 2004 presidential election, voting machines either malfunctioned, or were declared out of service on Election Day. Pennsylvania's switch to electronic voting systems led to long lines, and confused poll workers and voters on how to operate the machines.

South Carolina

There have been significant voting problems in recent elections in South Carolina. Voting machine problems are increasing in the state. In the 2008 presidential primary, there were voting machine failures in Horry County. Some voters were unable to vote because the electronic voting machines would not operate at all.[67] Similar voting problems occurred in the 2002 midterm elections. In Pickens County, two precincts could not produce accurate vote totals because of computer problems with the voting machines.[68] These voting problems compromised the elections in the state.

Texas

In the 2004 presidential election, several counties in Texas used new electronic voting machines, and voters and poll workers were confused about how to use the machines. In addition to the confusion some machines broke down and led to long lines at some polling places. In some counties voting machines reportedly did not record votes accurately. In the 2004 early voting, in Travis County, some voters reported attempts to vote a straight Democrat ticket, but when they reviewed their votes they found it recorded a vote for Bush as President and not for Kerry. In Harris County, "only four or five of twenty machines were being used and the machines were very slow, which caused some voters to leave altogether."[69]

Similar problems of machine miscounts occurred in the 2002 midterm elections. In Scurry County, electronic machines calculated two Republican candidates for commissioner with landslide victories. In a hand recount it was revealed that Democrats had won by a much larger lead, which overturned the election.[70] Voting machine problems created confusion and distrust of the election process and procedures.

Utah

Electronic voting machines in the 2004 presidential election, counted more votes than registered voters in some jurisdictions. The Associated Press reported that in Daggett County there were 947 voters, four times more than its population, according to the 2005 Census. The attorney general led an investigation into the election problem. There were also reported problems of delays at the polls because of malfunctioning voting machines. In the 2004 early voting in Utah County and Salt Lake City, voters were delayed by the faulty new electronic voting machines.[71] Common voting problems in different counties have prompted calls for more accurate voting systems.

Wisconsin

There were voting problems in the 2004 presidential election in Milwaukee. Voting machines did not work or they malfunctioned. An EP volunteer who monitored one precinct reported there was "a discrepancy between a ward's machine vote totals and the ward's count of actual votes. The machine had recorded 982 votes, while the ward books showed 971 votes."[72] There were numerous complaints from voters that voting machine counters did not advance when a new ballot was cast. Therefore, many voters may have been disenfranchised in the elections.

CONCLUSION

The examination of electronic voting machines nationwide in recent elections demonstrates these machines have proven to be inaccurate and unreliable. These faulty machines have affected the integrity of elections in far too many states. Unknown to most voters is the fact that voting machine problems and miscounts have been occurring in our electoral system for decades. Noted election reform activist, Beverly Harris, who studied voting machine problems for decades, noted malfunctions date back to 1971.[73] However, malfunctions and miscounts have increased in recent years with the sharp rise of electronic voting machines. One computer scientist summarized the current problems of miscounts with electronic voting machines as follows:

All of the internal mechanics of voting are hidden from the voter. A computer can easily display one set of votes on the screen for confirmation by the voter while recording entirely different votes in electronic memory, either because of a programming error or a malicious design. Almost all the DREs currently certified by state and local agencies have an "audit gap" between the voter's finger and the electronic or magnetic medium on which the votes are recorded. Because the ballot must remain secret, there's no way to check whether the votes were accurately recorded once the voter leaves the booth; neither the recorded vote nor the process of recording it can be directly observed. Consequently, the integrity of elections rests on blind faith in the vendors, their employees, inspection laboratories, and people who may have access—legitimate or illegitimate—to the machine software.[74]

The numerous incidents discussed in this chapter of unreliable voting machines that flipped or inaccurately recorded votes denied many citizens their constitutional right to vote. Citizens were also deprived of their franchise when voting machines did not record votes at all, or poll workers did not provide voters with provisional ballots when machines did not work. Provisions for problematic voting machines are established in several states. For example, New York provides for the use of a paper ballot if there is an electric problem. Some states such as Tennessee have emergency battery power if the electricity to power electronic voting machines was affected. Voters could also use paper ballots in such an emergency. However this study revealed many voters were not provided with provisional ballots or paper ballots when their precincts closed because of malfunctioning machines and when machines were declared out of service. Many voters left the polls without being able to vote in those emergencies, which diluted the vote in those jurisdictions.

Numerous lawsuits have been filed by voters in several states in which elections were compromised by malfunctioning machines. Election officials must be reminded that "the right of suffrage can be denied by a debasement or dilution of the weight of a citizen's vote just as effectively as by wholly prohibiting the free exercise of the franchise."[75] The U.S. Supreme Court has stated in several cases that if voters are unable to cast a ballot when their intent is to do so, then in essence, the franchise is denied to those voters. The common occurrences of voting machine malfunctions in about half the states indicate electronic voting systems are more than unreliable; they deny the franchise and affect the integrity of elections.

Chapter 3

How Secure are America's Voting Machines? Controversy and Misperceptions

Paperless electronic voting machines cannot be made secure.
Assessment by the National Institute of Standards & Technology

Electronic voting machines, first introduced in the 1970s, have progressively developed into a technologically advanced voting system. The advancement in the 1990s of this computerized voting technology was viewed as an improvement in the election process. It was also promoted by the Help America Vote Act as an upgrade to the process of casting and counting ballots. This led to increase usage of electronic voting machines in elections nationwide. In the 2008 presidential election, for the first time in the United States' history, more Americans used electronic voting machines. Consequently, as the utilization of electronic voting systems increases there is grave concern about their security.

Critics suggest the election could be compromised by electronic voting machines that are prone to tampering, hacking, and fraud. Computer scientists believe because the programming of voting machines used nationwide is secret, insiders could program the voting system to alter election results without detection. Another security criticism is the proliferation of electronic voting systems without verifiable paper trial to audit or recount election results.

The concerns about the security of electronic machines evolved after several studies in 2003 illustrated various security weaknesses with the voting systems. The questions about their security have led to a firestorm of debate and controversy. However, voters lack a clear understanding about the problems as they relate to the security of their votes. In an effort to clarify and enlighten voters about the security threats, this chapter answers the common questions:[1] Are electronic voting systems at risk to being hacked? Could electronic voting machine software be programmed to change the outcome of election results? Are electronic voting machines more vulnerable to fraud than other types of voting machines? Which states do not have a verifiable paper trail that could affect whether votes are counted in those jurisdictions? Which elections have been compromised because of no paper trail? An assessment of the major studies on the security of voting machines will provide the answers to these questions and demonstrate the security vulnerabilities of electronic voting machines.

UNIQUE SECURITY PROBLEMS

Electronic voting systems are the most technologically advanced of all voting systems. These voting machines, therefore, present a more unique security threat than other voting systems.

While the optical scan or punch-card counter could also be programmed to record a different vote from that intended by the voter, with those systems the ballot that the voter saw is preserved as part of normal practice and can be checked independently by another machine or a human. That is not possible with a DRE, where the choices the voter sees on the face of the machine are ephemeral—they are reset when the voter casts the ballot.[2]

Tampering with electronic voting systems can occur without detections, unlike other voting machines. "The difference is that any tampering with lever machines would have to be done one machine at a time, whereas malicious code need be inserted into DRE software only once, before it is loaded onto the machines."[3] With the increase usage of electronic machines, scientists warn of potential undetectable security violations that threaten the integrity of election results. There is a recent example of poll workers who ignored some of the safeguards designed to help detect security violations. A reporter for the *New York Times Magazine* observed the following security errors of the poll workers:

When a touch-screen machine is turned on for the first time on Election Day, two observers from different parties are supposed to print and view the "zero tape" that shows there are no votes already recorded on the machine; a hacker could fix the vote by programming the machine to start, for example, with a negative total of votes for a candidate. Yet when I visited one Cleveland polling station at daybreak, the two checkers signed zero tapes without actually checking the zero totals. And then, of course there were server crashes, and the recording errors on 20 percent of the paper recount ballots.[4]

Electronic machines employ complicated software that is not openly tested in the scientific community. Manufacturers object to tests by the scientific community for proprietary and intellectual property reasons. The machines are, however, tested for federal and state certification by scientists who cannot disclose information about the technology to the public. The federal government plays a limited role in the manufacture of these machines.[5] It sets standards for features, controls, and performance, but these are not mandatory requirements. This fuels criticism leading many to believe the concerns and conspiracy theories will continue until there is more transparency of electronic machines.

MAJOR SECURITY STUDIES

Many scientists have noted in several studies that electronic machines could jeopardize election results, not only because of inadequate oversight, but unreliability, poor programming, and susceptibility to attacks. Studies by academics, government agencies, computer scientists, nonprofit organizations, and activists all found security vulnerabilities with the new electronic machines. These studies helped to bring attention to security problems that were not addressed by election officials. A close assessment of each of the major studies demonstrates the great security risks that electronic machines present in upcoming elections.

Hopkins Report

The most influential and significant security study that had a far reaching impact is the Hopkins study of 2003. This study set off the firestorm of national debate about the security of electronic machines. The study was conducted by computer scientists at John Hopkins and Rice University. They examined the unencrypted "source code" of the software that operates the Diebold AccuVote-TS voting machines. They were able to locate the source code because the manufacturer, who does not disclose its software, unintentionally left thousands of computer files, including program files, on an unprotected company site on the Internet.[6] The code was discovered by long-time activist Beverly Harris, who for years had critically questioned the security and reliability of electronic voting machines. The Hopkins study, Analysis of an Electronic Voting System, exposed a wide range of security flaws. The 24-page report was the first scientific piece of evidence that showed current touch-screen technology could be seriously flawed. They wrote the following:

> We identify several problems including unauthorized privilege esca-
> lation, incorrect use of cryptography, vulnerabilities to network threats,
> and poor software development processes. We show that voters, with-
> out any insider privileges, can cast unlimited votes without being
> detected by any mechanisms within the voting terminal software.
> Furthermore . . . we demonstrate that the insider threat is also quite
> considerable, showing that not only can an insider, such as a poll
> worker, modify the votes, but that insiders can also violate voter pri-
> vacy and match votes with the voters who cast them. We conclude
> that this voting system is unsuitable for use in a general election.[7]

The Hopkins study discovered that the software was also "poorly written." It found all the voting machines had the same "password hardwired into the code." The principal investigator of the study, Aviel Rubin, said a "teenager could easily create counterfeit smart cards" and vote numerous times undetected. The study noted the following:

> Voters can easily program their own smartcards to simulate the be-
> havior of valid smartcards used in the election. With such homebrew
> cards, a voter can cast multiple ballots without leaving any trace. A
> voter can also perform actions that normally require administrative
> privileges, including viewing partial results and terminating the elec-
> tion early. Similar undesirable modifications could be made by ma-
> levolent poll workers (or janitorial staff) with access to the voting
> terminals before the start of an election.[8]

Election results depend on the reliably and security of voting terminals. The study found many design errors in the voting terminals. The investi-gators made the following observations:

> The protocols used when the voting terminals communicate with
> their home base, both to fetch election configuration information and
> to report final election results, do not use cryptographic techniques
> to authenticate either end of the connection nor do they check the
> integrity of the data in transit. Given that these voting terminals could
> potentially communicate over insecure phone lines or even wireless
> Internet connections, even unsophisticated attackers can perform un-
> traceable "man-in-the-middle" attacks. We considered both the specific
> ways that the code uses cryptographic techniques and the general

software engineering quality of its construction. Neither provides us with any confidence of the system's correctness.[9]

The release of this study prompted former Iowa state elections official Doug Jones to inform the Hopkins researchers that he examined the Global Elections Management System software five years prior to the Hopkins study and found the same security problems, of which he informed the manufacturer and government officials. The Hopkins report led other researchers to further study the security of electronic machines. The findings of the report also played a pivotal role in compelling states to reevaluate their use of electronic voting machines. Some states have since overhauled their voting systems.

RABA Technology Study for Maryland

As a result of the Hopkins study, Maryland commissioned a test of its electronic machines in 2003. RABA Technologies conducted the study of Maryland's Diebold electronic voting machines and testified before the state legislature of its vulnerabilities for exploitations. It showed the voting machines were vulnerable to undetectable errors. The company simulated an attack on the machines and was able to break into the computer servers.[10] Although the study showed significant security risks, Maryland used the machines in the 2006 midterm elections, which was plagued with malfunctions.

Studies in Swing States

States such as Ohio and Colorado found critical problems in the security and reliability of their electronic machines. They have determined the electronic voting machines were not sufficiently secure for the 2008 presidential election and changed systems. Researchers in Colorado declared,

> [The] machines could be corrupted with magnets or with Treos and other similar handheld devices. Two types of Sequoia Voting Systems used in Denver and three other counties were decertified because of security weaknesses, including a lack of password protection. Equipment made by Election Systems and Software had programming errors.[11]

Another swing state, California, found critical security flaws in the accuracy of the machines. It also announced that the machines were unsuitable for elections.

In Florida, the Department of State commissioned an independent review of the source code for its ES&S iVotronic voting machines after problems occurred in the 2006 midterm elections. A team of eight computer scientists from Florida State University's Security and Assurance in Information Technology Laboratory examined the machines. The scientists declared in their 2007 report that, "It is possible that an outsider could trigger an attack and that once one machine is infected, the virus would spread from machine to machine though removable storage media without further attacker involvement."[12] The state has since abandoned the electronic machines it used in the 2006 midterm elections. As a result of these significant studies these swing states rushed to replace these electronic systems before the 2008 presidential primaries.

Other states that are not considered swing states also conducted studies. One of the most notable studies occurred in Emery County, Utah, in 2006. The security test was conducted by Black Box Voting, commissioned by the former Emery County Clerk Bruce Funk. Testers examined the state's Diebold voting system and found they could disable the system and even change tallied votes. The study showed other security flaws that included electrical plugs that could easily be disconnected from the electrical sockets and other vulnerabilities for exploitation by hackers. State officials did not replace the voting systems but instead worked to improve the security of the machines.[13]

Princeton Study

The Princeton study by computer scientists on the AccuVote-TS is one of the latest studies to show electronic voting machines present significant security risks. The unique aspect of this study is that it extends the Hopkins study. It constructed simulated demonstrations on how easy it is to steal votes. The most notable discoveries of the report are:

> AccuVote-TS machines are susceptible to voting-machine viruses—computer viruses that can spread malicious software automatically and invisibly from machine to machine during normal pre- and post-election activity. We have constructed a demonstration virus that spreads in this way, installing our demonstration vote-stealing program on every machine it infects. While some of these problems can be eliminated by improving Diebold's software, others cannot be remedied without replacing the machines' hardware. Changes to election procedures would also be required to ensure security.[14]

The report pointed out that the security of computer software is difficult to ensure because of the nature of computers, in which much of the troubleshooting is reactive, not proactive. The potential problems are known only after they occur. In democratic elections this is problematic because there is a 100 percent reliance on the system to work correctly and accurately at all times.

900 Computer Scientists' Petition

More than 900 experts in computer security and electronic voting have signed the online petition, "Resolution on Electronic Voting" declaring electronic voting systems are prone to tampering, malfunction, and programming error. Computer scientists charge that the software that runs the major electronic voting machines is riddled with security flaws. The coalition also strongly advocates for electronic voting equipments to have a voter-verifiable paper trail to help ensure the security of the machines.[15] A significant government study supports the recommendations of these nine hundred computer scientists.

National Institute of Standards & Technology Study

The assessment of electronic machines by the National Institute of Standards and Technology (NIST), a federal agency that advises the U.S. Election Assistance Commission, is significant because it is the first federal analysis of security vulnerabilities of electronic machines. NIST conducted their research by visiting and inspecting the testing laboratories of voting systems, interviewing state and local elections officials, election experts, and computer scientists with expertise in auditing, testing, and operations. The NIST researchers also volunteered as election judges and poll workers to observe the process of casting and counting ballots.[16] The study found the following:

> One conclusion drawn by NIST is that the lack of an independent audit capability in DRE voting systems is one of the main reasons behind continued questions about voting system security and diminished public confidence in elections. NIST does not know how to write testable requirements to make DREs secure, and NIST's recommendation to the STS [Security and Transparency Subcommittee] is that the DRE in practical terms cannot be made secure.[17]

The study also found that electronic voting systems by nature are software dependent which makes them more vulnerable than any other voting system to undetected programming errors or hidden codes.

> Voting systems that are software-dependent have no recourse but to rely on the correctness and integrity of their software in ways that software-independent systems do not. The need for software-independence in voting systems is based on the inability, in a practical sense, to test complex systems for errors and intentionally-introduced fraud. NIST's recommendation to the STS [Security and Transparency

Subcommittee of the Technical Guidelines Development Committee] - is that in practical terms the DRE's software-dependent approach cannot be made secure or highly reliable.[18]

This is the first significant study, independent of the computer science community, to acknowledge that the system is unreliable and insecure.[19] It recommends the following four ways to improve the voting system:

> The steps that would be needed to arrive at a secure software-dependent voting system would likely include the following: 1) Voting systems would have to be built to carefully vetted designs that include precise specifications of control and data inputs/outputs. 2) Voting system vendors would need to follow strict software development processes and prove their abilities to meet other strict standards of management and development. 3) Changes in the way voting systems are certified would be in order, including a requirement to perform fault analyses on the voting systems. 4) Changes in the way voting systems are maintained in the field would be necessary, especially in incorporating a feedback loop to the vendor for reporting errors and problems.[20]

It noted that the federal government would need to play an integral role in requiring these standards as well as the testing and certification of the machines.

All these significant studies brought to the forefront the security flaws and vulnerabilities of electronic voting machines. Although there are no substantiated reports of security breaches in recent elections, these studies consistently point out that vulnerabilities in the system could be exploited. These researchers were also in accord in their recommendations that one way to improve the security of electronic voting systems is to add a voter-verified paper audit feature.

VOTER-VERIFIED PAPER AUDIT TRAILS

Many election experts believe that because of the complexity with the electronic voting machine software, there should be a paper ballot, often referred to as voter-verified paper audit trail (VVPAT). Most electronic voting machines in various states leave no paper trail to ensure vote verification in a recount, or for voters to know their vote was correctly scanned. These paperless electronic voting machines are inconsistent with the checks and balances of a democratic society.

A VVPAT would provide transparency in the election. The lack of transparency in the manufacture, software, and programming of electronic machines has led some activists to call it the "black box," to signify the secret internal mechanics. Some activists and computer scientists have noted:

> All the internal mechanics of voting are hidden from the voter. A computer can easily display one set of votes on the screen for confirmation by the voter while recording entirely different votes in electronic memory, either because of a programming error or a malicious design. Almost all for the DREs . . . have an "audit gap" between the voter's finger and the electronic or magnetic medium on which the votes are recorded.[21]

There are numerous instances of voting machines displaying information on the computer screen for voters and its internal mechanics recorded different information. The 2002 runoff election in Florida provides a good example:

> A March 2002 runoff election in Wellington, FL, was decided by five votes, but 78 ballots had no recorded vote. Elections Supervisor Theresa LePore claimed those 78 people chose not to vote for the only office on the ballot! In 2000, a Sequoia DRE machine was taken out of service in an election in Middlesex County, NJ, after 65 votes had been cast. When the results were checked after the election, it was discovered that none of the 65 votes were recorded for the Democrat and Republican candidates for one office, even though 27 votes were each recorded for their running mates. A representative of Sequoia insisted that no votes were lost, and that voters had simply failed to cast votes for the two top candidates. Since there was no paper trail, it was impossible to resolve either question.[22]

Most of the criticism of electronic machines is owed to the secrecy of its process. In our democracy, the election process and procedures should be open so that threats to the process can be minimized.

The VVPAT would offer voters verifiability in the election process. It allows the voter to verify the ballot was not changed somewhere in the election process. Voters are able to verify the accuracy of the choices of candidates before the ballot is cast. It gives the voters the opportunity to compare the paper ballot with their choices on the computer screen. If there are differences, the ballot would be cancelled and a new ballot issued. In states that use the paper trail, legal disputes over election results are at a minimum. For example, in Leon County, Florida, one candidate in a recent election claimed his name was not on the ballot in one precinct.

After the election, the supervisor of elections examined the ballots and found:

> The name was there; the candidate was wrong . . . And that's what you can't do with (paperless) touch-screen technology. You could have never proven to that person's satisfaction that the screen didn't show his name. I like that certainty. The paper ends the discussion.[23]

The VVPAT would build voter confidence in the election process and procedures. Voter confidence has been declining in recent years as election debacles are highlighting the large percentage of rejected ballots of some voting systems. Additionally, there have been reports of "vote flipping" with the new electronic machines. The VVPAT gives the voter the opportunity to verify his or her vote and ensures him or her that the results of elections are verifiable. The paper trail gives the assurance to all Americans that every vote counts.[24]

There have been congressional deliberations about VVPAT that did not result in any laws mandating paper trails for all electronic voting machines. The lack of congressional action has led activists to focus on getting the states to adopt laws requiring mandatory VVPAT. California was the first state to mandate the VVPAT feature, and activists have been working to get other states to adopt similar regulations. Activist groups such as Voter Verified also strongly advocate for manual audits in randomly chosen precincts. This is another vote-verification method, which would compare the paper ballot to the votes recorded by the computer. About twenty-eight states require VVPAT on all electronic machines it purchases, and about thirteen also require the mandatory manual audit feature. Figure 3.1 shows the states that have not adopted VVPAT to ensure votes are counted, and the states that have implemented such requirements to protect the vote.

The VVPAT is not without opposition. The strongest opposition comes from state and local election officials, and manufacturers of electronic machines. They resist the implementation of VVPAT because "paper trails are a serious form of accountability in an area where there has been little of it. If the tallies in the paper trails do not match the totals on the machines, election offices and machine companies have to answer a lot of hard questions."[25] Opponents cite the added costs for this additional feature as deterrent to states with an already limited election budget. They also claim procedures for handling the paper ballots require additional training for poll workers already burdened with information. In addition, they point out that states that already use the paper ballots have made claims that some voters do not take the time to verify their votes. However, a paper trail is a record that protects the voter, if the machine were to malfunction,

Figure 3.1 Voter-Verified Paper Audit Trail and Mandatory Manual Audits

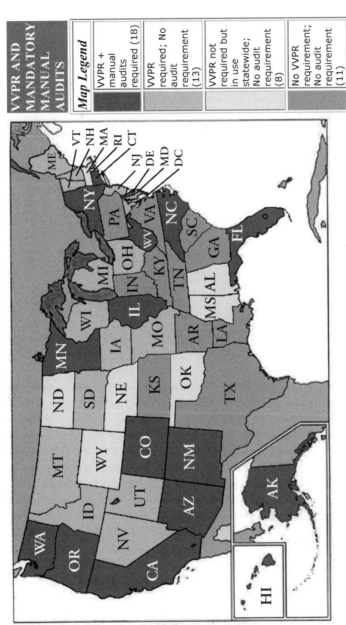

Source: VerifiedVoting.org—http://verifiedvoting.org. Last visited October 3, 2008.[26]
Note: VVPR = Voter-Verified Paper Record

and in the event of a recount the paper trail could be compared to the electronic total.

RECOUNTS AND AUDITS

Electronic machines, without recount capabilities, pose significant problems to our democracy. What if the margin of victory was close in the upcoming presidential election in many states and there was no paper trail to recount the results? Election recounts are essential safeguards of the election process in many states, as became evident in the 2000 Florida presidential recount efforts. Some states require, by law, certain recount procedures in a close race. Several recent examples indicate that those states will be unable to conduct a recount from electronic voting machines with no paper trail. For example, Cuyahoga County, Ohio, would have been unable to perform a complete recount in the 2006 midterm election because some machines crashed. The county commissioned a study by the Election Science Institute and discovered that about 10 percent of the paper records were blank or unreadable.[27] As a result the county has switched from using electronic voting machines after spending about $21 million for the touchscreens. The Ohio secretary of state issued a report in 2007 that touch-screen voting machines threatened the integrity of the election process.

There are specific examples of midterm elections that were compromised due to electronic machines without recount capabilities. In Sarasota County, Florida's 13th U.S. Congressional District contest in the 2006 midterm election, about eighteen thousand votes were missing from the ES&S iVotronic touch-screen machines. There was a 368-vote difference between the candidates, and there was no paper trail to audit the result. There was a 13 percent undervote in only that race, which the normal undervote in any given race is less than 3 percent according to election experts. The ES&S iVotronic voting system records votes on a removable flash memory card stored in the touch-screen voting machine and has no paper trail for a recount. To comply with Florida's recount law for close races, election officials simply "printed" a hard copy of the information stored on the flash memory card, which could not explain the missing votes.[28] Computer scientists have long advocated for the paper trail because it provides verifiability of voters and:

> Because the ballot must remain secret, there's no way to check whether the votes were accurately recorded once the voter leaves the booth; neither the recorded vote nor the process of recording it can be directly observed. Consequently, the integrity of elections rests on blind faith in the vendors, their employees, inspection laboratories, and people who may have access—legitimate or illegitimate—to the machine software.[29]

Audits have also added another protective security component that compliments recount efforts. Although recounts focus on the printed ballots, audits provide an in-depth assessment of the voting process, including the internal mechanics of voting equipment, the counting procedures, and election totals. Paperless electronic machines deny states of this protective security measure that was instituted as a safeguard for election integrity.

In numerous reports, electronic machines presented critical problems that affected recount efforts. An audit of the electronic voting machines in 2006 in Cuyahoga County, Ohio, showed that for about "72.5 percent of the audited machines, the paper trail did not match the digital tally on the memory cards."[30] In addition, several machines had printers that jammed, which therefore could not produce a paper trail. In other states, machines flipped votes for other candidates, counted backward, or deleted votes.[31] One report stated, "Problems with electronic voting last November rang[ed] from software glitches that cause votes to be counted twice to faulty memory cartridge and caused votes to be added to races in which they were not cast."[32] In a 2006 mayoral race in Waldenburg, Arkansas, the machines recorded no votes, in a town of 80 residents. A mayoral candidate said that he voted for himself.[33]

The security of voting machines has become one of the most contentious and divisive aspects of the modern election process. The VVPAT offers one of the best solutions against the mount of security vulnerabilities. Many Americans will use electronic voting machines in the next presidential election, and they should be able to have confidence in the election results. Will voters accept a presidency decided by voting machines with questionable security flaws or entangled in a cloud of widespread security suspicion? America will be at a pivotal moment in its democracy, if the security of its voting machines is ever called into question in a presidential election.[34]

Chapter 4

Vote Dilution: An Analysis of Voting Irregularities

Those who cast the votes decide nothing. Those who count the votes decide everything.

Joseph Stalin, Communist Dictator

Presidential elections of recent years have been tainted by reports of eligible voters being turned away from the polls because of voter intimidation, discrimination, improper voter purges, problems at the polls, and registration errors. Perhaps the most crippling aspect of America's electoral system is the disenfranchisement of thousands of voters. Every election in this decade has had reports of voting irregularities at the polls. This investigation found voting problems in the 2008 presidential primaries and the 2004 and 2000 presidential elections that disproportionately affected minorities in the casting and counting of their ballots in various states.

The personal testimonies and complaints of citizens collected in public hearings and hotlines (toll-free numbers) concerning disenfranchisement show common claims of voting irregularities in every election this decade. More important, the voting problems in the 2000, 2004, and 2008 presidential elections are similar problems that led to the Voting Rights Act of the 1960s and 1980s. These recent incidents of voting irregularities make it clear difficulties persist with universal suffrage, long after the enactment of the 1965 Voting Rights Act. This chapter presents research findings of voting irregularities in every election this decade. The disenfranchisement of voters poses a significant threat to our democracy.

2008 PRESIDENTIAL PRIMARIES

In the highly contested 2008 presidential election various voting rights and advocacy groups teamed up to collect public testimonies of voting irregularities at the polls. They monitored elections, staffed phone lines to assist voters, obtained court orders to extend polling hours, and filed lawsuits challenging various aspects of election procedures. Election Activists, civil and voting rights groups such as the National Association for the Advancement of Colored People (NAACP), the American Civil Liberties Union (ACLU), People for the American Way, the National Coalition on Black Civic Participation, the Lawyers' Committee for Civil Rights Under Law, Election Protection Coalition, the Tom Joyner Radio Morning Show, and many more, teamed up to establish and operate toll-free numbers (hotlines) for voters on Election Day to report voting problems.

The Tom Joyner Radio Show and the NAACP National Voter Fund partnered to operate the national hotline 1-866-MYVOTE-1 for voters to report voting irregularities. Joyner testified at a Congressional hearing on April 9, 2008, to the House Administration Committee, which oversees elections, about the voter complaints collected from the 1-866-MYVOTE-1 hotline. The toll-free number was used by voters nationwide and operated until the 2008 general election. During the 2008 presidential primaries the hotline received about forty-five thousand calls with more than twenty thousand calls about polling locations, and about four thousand complaints about problems at polling sites. Voters also reported problems with voting machines and inadequately trained poll workers that could not fix the machine problems. On Super Tuesday they received about ten thousand calls and "at one point [they] received up to three calls a minute."[1]

The Election Protection (EP) Coalition, a coalition of about forty organizations also established a toll-free phone line for voters to report voting problems. The 1-866-OUR–VOTE hotline collected tens of thousands of voter complaints in elections this decade. They established about eight call centers nationwide at law firms where volunteer lawyers staffed over one hundred phone lines. There is also an affiliated Spanish-language line, monitored by the National Association of Latino Elected Officials. During the 2008 presidential primaries 1-866-OUR–VOTE hotline received thousands of calls from the first forty-three states and the District of Columbia that had their primaries.[2]

The coalition prepared a multifaceted strategy to monitor the 2008 Election Day.

As November [2008 general election] draws closer, the Lawyers' Committee is gearing up to provide the most extensive legal assistance structure to its Election Protection allies since the founding of the program in 2001. Ten thousand legal volunteers will form over

25 local Election Protection Legal Committees (EPCLs) to provide comprehensive legal assistance, guidance, support and advice to diverse coalitions of state and local voter mobilization partners, answer over 200,000 calls to the 866-OUR-VOTE Hotline . . . There will be more call centers, more trained volunteers and more locations to provide immediate assistance to voters.[3]

EP also collected public statements from their hotlines and public hearings from the 2004 presidential election and the 2006 midterm election. Its study, "2004 Shattering the Myth: An Initial Snapshot of Voter Disenfranchisement in the 2004 Elections," reported more than thirty-nine thousand complaints during the 2004 presidential election, and the 2008 presidential primary report "Looking Ahead to November" captured the most recent testimonies from voters. Appendix A provides excerpts from their reports of voter irregularities in the 2004 presidential election, and 2008 presidential primaries.

2004 PRESIDENTIAL ELECTION

Civil and voting rights organizations and political parties sent monitors to various states during the 2004 election to observe the activities at polling sites. These organizations captured numerous incidents of intimidation at predominately low-income and minority precincts. They documented hundreds of voting irregularities at public hearings and interviewed election officials.

Election Protection Coalition Hearings

The first public hearing after the 2004 presidential election was led by the EP Coalition. A series of public hearings were planned in at least eight states: Ohio, Florida, Pennsylvania, Arizona, Michigan, New Mexico, Colorado, and Texas. The first public hearing was held in Columbus, Ohio. On November 13 and 15, 2005, the EP Coalition received personal testimonies from about thirty-two Ohio voters, precinct judges, poll workers, legal observers, and party challengers. In addition, about sixty-six people wrote affidavits about election irregularities. The hearings in Columbus received testimonies of discrimination and confusion. Among them were the following testimonies from residents in the state:[4]

Werner Lange, a pastor from Youngstown, Ohio, said:

In precincts 1 A and 5 G, voting as Hillman Elementary School, which is a predominantly African American community, there were woefully insufficient number of voting machines in three precincts. I was

told that the standard was to have one voting machine per 100 registered voters. Precinct A had 750 registered voters. Precinct G had 690.
There should have been fourteen voting machines at this site. There
were only six, three per precinct, less than 50 percent of the standard.
This caused an enormous bottleneck among voters who had to wait a
very, very long time to vote, many of them giving up in frustration
and leaving. . . . I estimate, by the way, that an estimated loss of over
8,000 votes from the African American community in the City of
Youngstown alone, with its 84 precincts, were lost due to insufficient
voting machines, and that would translate to some 7,000 votes lost for
John Kerry for President in Youngstown alone.

Boyd Mitchell, Columbus:

What I saw was voter intimidation in the form of city employees that
were sent in to stop illegal parking. Now, in Driving Park Rec Center
there are less than fifty legal parking spots, and there were literally
hundreds and hundreds of voters there, and I estimated at least
70 percent of the people were illegally parked in the grass around the
perimeter of the Driving Park Rec Center, and two city employees
drove up in a city truck and said that they had been sent there to stop
illegal parking, and they went so far as to harass at least a couple of
voters that I saw . . . And I saw fifteen people who left because the
line was too long. The lines inside were anywhere from 2 1/2 to
5 hours. Most everybody said 4 hours, and I saw at least fifteen people who did not vote.

Joe Popich (entered into the record copies of the Perry County Board
of Election poll book):

There are a bunch of irregularities in this log book, but the most
blatant irregularity would be the fact that there are 360 signatures in
this book. There are thirty-three people who voted absentee ballot at
this precinct, for a total of 393 votes that should be attributed to that
precinct. However, the Board of Elections is attributing ninety-six
more votes to that precinct than what this log book reflects.

Carol Shelton, presiding judge, precinct 25 B at the Linden Branch of
the Columbus Metropolitan Library:

The precinct is 95 to 99 percent black. . . . There were 1,500 persons
on the precinct rolls. We received three machines. In my own precinct
in Clintonville, 19E, we always received three machines for 700 to

730 voters. Voter turnout in my own precinct has reached as high as 70 percent while I worked there. I interviewed many voters in 25 B and asked how many machines they had in the past. Everyone who had a recollection said five or six. I called to get more machines and ended up being connected with Matt Damschroder, the Director of the Board of Elections. After a real hassle—and someone here has it on videotape, he sent me a fourth machine which did not dent the length of the line. Fewer than 700 voted, although the turnout at the beginning of the day would cause anyone to predict a turnout of over 80 percent. This was a clear case of voter suppression by making voting an impossibility for anyone who had to go to work or anyone who was stuck at home caring for children or the elderly while another family member voted.

Allesondra Hernandez, Toledo:

What I witnessed when I had gotten there about 9 A.M. was a young African American woman who had come out nearly in tears. She was a new voter, first registered, very excited to vote, and she had said that she had been bounced around to three different polling places, and this one had just turned her down again. People were there to help her out, and I was concerned. I started asking around to everyone else, and they had informed me earlier that day that she was not the only one, but there were at least three others who had been bounced around.

Erin Deignan, Columbus:

I was an official poll worker judge in precinct Columbus 25 F, at the East Linden School. We had between 1,100 and 1,200 people on the voter registry there. We had three voting machines. We did the math. I am sure lots of other people did too. With the five-minute limit, 13 hours the polls were open, three machines, that is 468 voters, that is less than half of the people we had on the registry. We stayed open three hours past 7:30 and got about 550 people through, but we had one Board of Elections worker come in the morning. We asked if he could bring more machines. He said more machines had been delivered, but they didn't have any more. We had another Board of Elections official come later in the day, and he said that in Upper Arlington he had seen 12 machines.

Matthew Segal, Gambier:

Kenyon students and the residents of Gambier had to stand in line up to 10 to 12 hours in the rain, through a hot gym, and crowded narrow lines, making it extremely uncomfortable. As a result of this, voters were disenfranchised, having class to attend to, sports commitments, and midterms for the next day, which they had to study for. Obviously, it is a disgrace that kids who are being perpetually told the importance of voting, could not vote because they had other commitments and had to be put up with a 12-hour line.

In addition to collecting testimonies at public hearings the Election Protection Coalition also sent about twenty-five thousand volunteers, which included more than eight thousand lawyers, to observe more than thirty-five thousand precincts nationwide. They monitored predominately African American, Latino, and low-income precincts. They also analyzed more than thirty-nine thousand voter complaints recorded in the Electronic Incident Reporting System (EIRS) database. The report contained incidents of voter suppression or intimidation at the polls such as:

> Police stationed outside a Cook County, Illinois, polling place requesting photo ID and telling voters if they had been convicted of a felony that they could not vote. In Arizona, voters at multiple polls were confronted by an individual wearing a black tee shirt with "U.S. Constitution Enforcer" and a military-style belt that gave the appearance he was armed. He asked voters if they were citizens, accompanied by a cameraman who filmed the encounters. Misinformation campaigns delivered through anonymous flyers or phone calls with a variety of intimidating or vote-suppressing messages, advising voters to go to the polls on November 3rd rather than November 2, or giving other false information on voting rights.[5]

The EP Coalition also found extensive evidence of voting irregularities in the 2004 presidential election in the following seventeen states: Florida, Ohio, Pennsylvania, Arizona, Michigan, Wisconsin, New Mexico, Illinois, Colorado, Minnesota, Nevada, Missouri, Texas, North Carolina, Louisiana, Georgia, and Arkansas. They found there was a lack of adequate resources such as insufficient voting machines and election officials to administer the election. Most of the reported problems involved voter registration, absentee ballots, machine errors, voter suppression or intimidation, and provisional ballots. The EP Coalition concluded these voting problems led to extraordinarily long lines that discouraged some people from voting and may have diluted the vote.

U.S. House Judiciary Committee Study

Representative John Conyers, Jr., the ranking democrat on the House Judiciary Committee, conducted an investigation on the irregularities in the Ohio 2004 presidential election. In January 2005, the final report detailed findings of numerous cases of election irregularities in Ohio. They found widespread incidents of intimidation, misinformation, and improper purging that disenfranchised thousands of voters—which violated the Voting Rights Act, the Civil Rights Act of 1968, Equal Protection and Due Process clauses, and Ohio's statutes:

> The Greater Cleveland Voter Registration Coalition projects that in Cuyahoga County alone over 10,000 Ohio citizens lost their right to vote as a result of official registration errors. There were 93,000 spoiled ballots where no vote was cast for president, the vast majority of which have yet to be inspected. The problem was particularly acute in two precincts in Montgomery County which had an under vote rate of over 25 percent each—accounting for nearly 6,000 voters who stood in line to vote, but purportedly declined to vote for president.[6]

The investigation also held the Secretary of State Kenneth Blackwell as responsible for most of the voting problems in the state. It reported, in part, "Mr. Blackwell's decision to restrict provisional ballots resulted in the disenfranchisement of tens, if not hundreds of thousands of voters, again predominantly minority and Democratic voters."[7] The Committee's investigation also presented voting irregularities in specific counties in the state.

> In Mahoning county, at least twenty-five electronic machines transferred an unknown number of Kerry votes to the Bush column; (ii) Warren County locked out public observers from vote counting, citing an FBI warning about a potential terrorist threat, yet the FBI states that it issued no such warning; (iii) the voting records of Perry County showed significantly more votes than voters in some precincts, significantly less ballots than voters in other precincts, and voters casting more than one ballot; (iv) in Butler County a down ballot and underfunded Democratic State Supreme Court candidate implausibly received more votes than the best funded Democratic Presidential candidate in history; (v) in Cuyahoga County, poll worker errors may have led to little known third party candidates receiving twenty times more votes than such candidates had ever received in otherwise reliably Democratic leaning areas; (vi) in Miami County, voter turnout was an improbable and highly suspect 98.55 percent, and after 100 percent of the precincts were reported, an additional 19,000 extra votes were recorded for President Bush.[8]

These findings of the House Judiciary Committee are consistent with the investigation of another election monitoring organization Count the Vote. The organization sent monitors to seven hundred precincts in twenty-seven counties in Ohio, Alabama, Florida, Georgia, Louisiana, Mississippi, North Carolina, and South Carolina. Count the Vote found numerous factors that led to voting irregularities including limited voting machines in counties such as Duval County, which is the largest county in Florida. It also found that voting conditions deterred voters from voting. Elections monitor Alma Ayala who monitored polling places in St. Petersburg, Florida, observed, "In one case, sprinklers came on while people were waiting to vote and the poll workers didn't know how to turn them off."[9] The report also noted in three South Carolina counties there were several machine malfunctions of electronic voting machines. The Count the Vote investigation of irregularities was a joint effort with the NAACP National Voter Fund, the Women of Color Resource Center, the National Coalition on Black Civic Participation, American Human Rights Foundation, and other organizations in North Carolina, South Carolina, Georgia, Florida, Alabama, Mississippi, and Louisiana.

The problems that occurred in the 2004 election also occurred in the 2000 election. Minority voters faced similar barriers to cast a ballot in both presidential elections.

2000 PRESIDENTIAL ELECTION

Accusations of voting irregularities in the 2000 election surfaced early Election Day as many eligible African American voters claimed they were prevented from voting for the candidate of their choice.[10] In fact, the first set of complaints on Election Day was voting irregularities from African American voters in Florida.[11] Complaints were also filed by voters in several other states.[12] Table 4.1 demonstrates the cases that were filed in Florida alone.

Incidents of voting irregularities were reported to various civil rights organizations,[13] the Democratic and Republican parties, as well as the Florida attorney general's office. "The Florida attorney general's office alone received more than 3,600 allegations, 2,600 complaints, and 1,000 letters."[14] The U.S. Justice Department received more than eleven thousand complaints from voters after the 2000 election.[15] In addition to the complaints filed, testimonies were collected at public hearings held by the Congressional Black Caucus, the Florida Legislature, the NAACP, and the U.S. Commission on Civil Rights. The latter two collected the most extensive evidence of disenfranchisement. Appendix B provides excerpts of some of the public testimonies.

NAACP Public Hearings

The NAACP held the first public hearing on voting irregularities in Florida. On November 11, 2000, the NAACP held a hearing in Miami to

Table 4.1 Major Voting Irregularities Cases in Florida in the 2000
          Presidential Election

Cases	Issue
Horowitz v. Lepore	Voting irregularities
Elkin v. Lepore	Voting irregularities
Gottfried v. LePore	Voting irregularities
Haitian American Bureau and Int'l Liaison v. Palm Beach County Board	Voting irregularities
Gibbs v. Palm Beach County Board	Voting irregularities
Brown v. Staffard	Voting irregularities
Roger v. Election Canvassing Commission of Florida	Voting irregularities
Crum v. Palm Beach County Canvassing Board	Voting irregularities
Litchman v. Bush	Voting irregularities
Katz v. Florida Election Canvassing Board	Voting irregularities

Source: Compiled by Percy (2003).

investigate violations of the Voting Rights Act and interviewed witnesses. It took testimonies from voters, poll workers, and the volunteers it sent to observe voting irregularities on Election Day, when it began receiving complaints. Many people testified that polling sites moved or closed early, lacked resources, or were of poor condition—affecting voting on Election Day. Several voters testified they reported to their designated precincts where they had voted for years and found the location was moved without notification from the county supervisor of elections. Public testimonials included various problems such as the following:

Donnise Desouza testified:

We got there (polling place) at 6:30 to find a long line of cars with Metro-Dade County Police Officers directing traffic . . . We do finally get to park at ten minutes to 7:00 . . . I showed the poll worker my identification . . . and he said, 'we have a problem. You're not on the rolls.' He said you need to go to this other line . . . So 7:00 o'clock comes, and they start closing the doors and shutting people out as one of the administrator's said to us, "I'm sorry, but if your name is not on the roll, you cannot vote." There were people there with their identification, with their voter's registration cards, and we couldn't vote.[16]

Andree Berkowitz, who is white, observed:

They did not ask me at all for a photo ID, however, they did ask the African Americans that were voting for photo ID's. I did see people being turned away when they claimed they were registered voters and (they) were not on the list to sign in to vote . . . I was there for a good forty-five minutes time (and) there was not one inspector that offered to assist any of these voters that were turned away, not one.[17]

Dymon Raimer testified of voter registration problems:

Around early or mid September, I sent in my (voter registration) application. By October 6th or 7th I received a letter from them saying that my registration was invalid due to the fact that I put my P.O. Box as my mailing address . . . So, about a day later . . . I sent it in. I went down there (polls) on the 7th . . . they said my name wasn't on the list . . . The lady (poll worker) made a phone call to the courthouse and she said my registration was completed and it went through, but it was on hold because they received it two days later. [18]

Katreece Dunbar witnessed:

I noticed several people being asked to provide voter registration cards as well as a picture ID in order to vote. Even though they had these types of identification they were told that they could not vote because they were not on the books. They were told to stand aside, there were a lot people at this particular polling site and basically they were literally left standing there because no one could help them.[19]

The NAACP concluded from the public hearings that the 2000 Florida presidential election violated the Equal Protection and Due Process Clauses of the Fourteenth Amendment; the Privileges and Immunities Clause of the Fourteenth Amendment to the U.S. Constitution; the National Voter Registration Act, and 42 U.S.C. §1983; Section 2 of the Voting Rights Act of 1965, Civil Rights Act of 1957 and 1960 (42 U.S.C. §1971); and Florida's civil rights laws. On January 10, 2001, the NAACP joined with other advocacy groups and filed *NAACP v. Harris* challenging discriminatory voting practices for African Americans in Florida.[20]

U.S. Commission on Civil Rights Hearings

The U.S. Commission on Civil Rights (the Commission) conducted hearings in Florida on January 11–12, 2001, in Tallahassee and on February 16, 2001, in Miami.[21] The Commission used its subpoena powers to receive more than thirty hours of testimonies from more than 100 citizens, and examined more than 118,000 pages of documents.[22] The Commission took a wide array of testimonies from voters under oath. For example, Susan and Joe Newman testified about the early closure of their polling place. They said they tried to vote at the Water Works Department in Palm Beach at 6:15 P.M. and could not enter the polling site because the iron gate was locked.

> Several cars pulled into the entrance landing and tried to attract attention honking horns and ringing an intercom. We waited 5–10 minutes but no one showed up and the gates remained locked. We drove off thinking we were wrong about the closing time . . . A few blocks away we spotted a police car and pulled up to check. He verified that the polls were open till 7 P.M. We complained about the situation we had just experienced and he told us to go to the Boards of Elections. We drove there and met a policeman and we entered the building. He told us (Theresa Lepore's) office closed at 5 P.M., her staff went home, and we would have to complain the following day.[23]

Many Floridians testified they were registered to vote through the Department of Highway Safety and Motor Vehicle program and discovered on Election Day their names were not placed on the registration list to vote. Poll worker, Maria Desoto, testified about registration and polling problems she witnessed:

> There were people who had registered to vote through motor voter and somehow their registration was not transmitted to the supervisor of elections office. I saw that with married couples in my own precinct. One person would be registered to vote and the other couldn't vote unless they physically went to the supervisor of elections office and picked up a piece of paper, which they then brought back to me, because we couldn't reach them on the telephone. It was incredibly confusing and frustrating that day. The machines were all jamming . . . It was a mess.[24]

The Commission's hearings revealed common occurrences of voting irregularities on Election Day including the following: failure to notify voters of polling place closures or relocation, registered voters were not on the voter lists, no voter verification from the supervisor of elections on the registration rolls, citizens were incorrectly purged from the voter lists, lack of assistance for disabled and language minorities, and police presence intimidated voters. The Commission published a report of its findings on the 2000 election[25] as well as an elections reform manual.[26] The conclusion of the Commission's investigation was that "many eligible Florida voters were, in fact, denied their right to vote, with the disenfranchisement disproportionately affecting African Americans."[27] It urged the Justice Department and the Civil Rights Division in the office of the Florida attorney general to prosecute state election officials whose actions violated federal and state laws.[28]

The public hearings of The Commission and the NAACP identified the irregularities in the casting of the ballot in the 2000 election. Other organizations extended the body of knowledge on irregularities in the election by conducting studies that revealed irregularities also transpired in the counting of the ballots.

Rejected Ballots

Several studies discovered a high rejection rate of African American ballots in the 2000 election. Studies by the Florida Governor's Select Task Force on Election Procedures, Standards, and Technology and The Commission revealed that voters who were able to cast a ballot were perhaps later disenfranchised in the counting of those ballots. The high spoilage rate of ballots in Florida may be attributed, in part, to the voting systems in each county and varying budgets. Other studies point out that citizens in poorer, predominantly black communities were more likely to use voting systems with higher spoilage rates. Analysis showed that Democrats were more likely to live in counties that used punch cards. The study concluded the following:

> The impact of these differences on the outcome will never be known but their potential magnitude is evident in Miami-Dade County, where predominantly black precincts saw their vote thrown out at twice the rate as Hispanic precincts and nearly four times the rate of white precincts. In all, one out of eleven ballots in predominantly black precincts were rejected, a total of 9,904.[29]

In the 2000 Florida presidential election, African American voters were about ten times more likely than non-black voters to cast spoiled ballots. Figure 4.1 illustrates the spoiled ballots of the 2000 Florida presidential election, revealing the high spoilage rate of votes cast by African American voters. About 14.4 percent of African American ballots were rejected, while about 1.6 percent of non-black voters' ballots were rejected. African Americans make up about 11 percent of Florida's voting population but cast about 54 percent of the 180,000 spoiled ballots in the election.[30]

The *Miami Herald* and *USA Today* conducted an analysis of Florida's black precincts and found considerable disparities between majority black

Figure 4.1 The Spoiled Ballots of Florida Voters in the 2000 Presidential
          Election

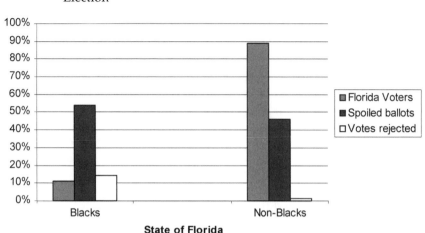

Source: Figure compiled by Percy (2003). Voting data based on Governor's Select
Task Force, *Revitalizing Democracy* (Tallahassee, Florida: The Collins Center for
Public Policy, 2001); The U.S. Commission on Civil Rights, *Voting Irregularities in
Florida During the 2000 Presidential Election* (Washington, DC: U.S. Government
Printing Office, 2001).

precincts and majority white precincts. The study reviewed 5,775 precincts
and compared the amount of rejected ballots with the precincts' racial
makeup. The study revealed the following:

> In majority-black precincts, 8.9 percent of votes cast were uncounted.
> In majority-white precincts, 2.4 percent of votes cast were uncounted.
> Among the 100 precincts with the highest numbers of disqualified
> ballots, 83 of them were majority African American precincts. Fifty-
> seven of them are in Duval County alone. Thirteen of 15 precincts
> with the highest percentage of spoiled ballots were majority-black in
> Duval County, which used punch-card ballots.[31]

Another study conducted by the *Washington Post* on precinct-by-
precinct analysis substantiated the findings of The *Miami Herald* and *USA
Today*. The *Post* reported the analysis of election returns indicated that the
more black and Democratic the precinct the more likely it was to have a
high rejection rate of ballots. "In the most heavily white precincts, about
1 in 14 ballots were thrown out, but in largely black precincts more than 1
in 5 ballots were spoiled—and in some black precincts it was almost one-
third."[32] The study also found that African Americans were more likely to

reside in precincts where poll workers were not properly trained to provide instructions, check ballots for errors, or provide answers concerning the confusion ballots. The study found the following:

> The three counties Gore asked to be recounted—Palm Beach, Broward and Miami-Dade—had 72,000 invalidated ballots . . . key reason the Bush campaign did not ask for a statewide recount was it feared that Gore would pick up more votes than Bush, because of the high rate of ballot spoilage in black precincts.[33]

The *Post* also determined that certain precincts in Miami-Dade where less than "30 percent of the voters are black, about 3 percent of ballots did not register a vote for president. In precincts where more than 70 percent of the voters are African Americans, it was nearly 10 percent."[34]

These studies indicated that different voting standards resulted in disparate treatment of voters in the same precincts. "Nine of the ten counties with the highest percentage of African American voters had spoilage rates above Florida average."[35] For example, Gadsden County had the highest spoilage rate in the state and is the only county with an African American majority. As depicted in Figure 4.2, Gadsden County, with 63 percent African American voters, used an optical central tabulation system and had a spoilage rate of 12.4 percent. One in eight votes in Gadsden was rejected. In Leon County, where blacks only make up 28 percent of the electorate, just two votes in one thousand were rejected.[36] Leon County used an optical precinct tabulation system, and the spoilage rate was only 0.18 percent,[37] the lowest spoilage rate in the state. "Of the ten counties with the highest percentage of white voters, only two counties had spoilage rates above the state average."[38]

These various studies support the findings of the public hearings of the NAACP and The Commission that African Americans in the 2000 election were disenfranchised in the casting of their ballots and in having their ballots counted.

LITIGATION

The various findings of voting irregularities in this decade led civil and voting rights organizations to bring due process and equal protection claims before the court. Individual voters also challenged electronic machines that they claimed disenfranchised citizens. For example, the court in *Stewart v. Blackwell* found that Ohio's use of punch-card ballots in some counties and electronic machine in other counties violated the Voting Rights Act as well as Ohio voters' equal protection and due process rights.[39] In *Wexler v. Florida*, voters argued that in some Florida counties some voters were

Figure 4.2 Rejected Ballots in the 2000 Presidential Election, Gadsden
        County, Florida

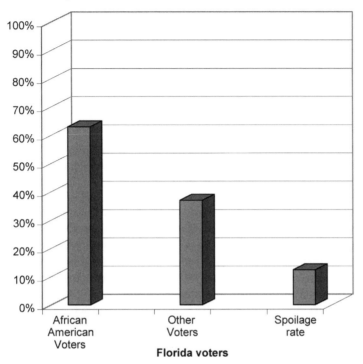

Source: Figure compiled by Percy (2003). Voting data based on The U.S.
Commission on Civil Rights, *Voting Irregularities in Florida During the 2000
Presidential Election* (Washington, DC: U.S. Government Printing Office, 2001).

unconstitutionally disenfranchised because the machines did not allow
for a meaningful manual recount in close elections, as required by Florida
law.[40] In another case *White v. Blackwell*, voters claimed the different voting
standards, inadequate training of poll workers and lack of voter education
disenfranchised citizens.[41] Other cases challenging equal access and voter
participation of minorities included *ACLU v Brunner*, *ACORN v. Bysiewicz*,
NAMUDNO v. Gonzales, and *Gooden v. Worley*.[42]

VOTING RIGHTS VIOLATIONS

The 2000 and 2004 public hearings, studies, and litigations identified different voting standards, procedures, and practices in the same county that
disproportionately affected black communities in the casting and counting
of their ballots. This violates the Voting Rights Act provision that specifically

prohibits different voting standards, practices, and procedures in the same county. The Voting Rights Act, 42 U.S.C. § 1971 (a) (2) (A) states:

> No person acting under color of law shall in determining whether any individual is qualified under state law or laws to vote in any elections, apply any **standard, practice or procedure** different from the **standards, practices,** and **procedures** applied under such laws or laws to other individuals within the same county, parish, or similar political subdivision who have been found by state officials to be qualified to vote.[43]

The 2000 Florida presidential election, for example, was a clear violation of these stipulations. There were five different voting systems for voters to select the candidate of their choice. There were also different procedures to protect voters from the overvote problem. For example, many voters and poll workers testified they were unable to verify registration status with the Supervisor of Election's office because of inadequate telephone systems. But some counties had laptop computers to verify the accuracy of their precinct registration list against the master county registration database. Broward County had thirty-one laptop computers placed in its largest precincts on Election Day. Miami-Dade County had eighteen laptop computers, but they were placed in mostly Cuban American voting precincts. The supervisor of elections David Leahy admitted only one laptop computer was located at a largely African American precinct.[44]

This investigation discovered some African Americans in recent presidential elections could not vote for the candidate of their choice because of confusing ballots, voting machine malfunctions, poll workers who voted for the elderly and Haitians when they asked for assistance, denial of language assistance to identify the candidate of choice, voting systems with broken stylus, inferior voting system with a high rejection rate, and individuals who made mistakes with the ballot and were denied another ballot to correctly mark the candidate of their choice. Table 4.2 identifies the common kinds of voting irregularities expressed at each hearing about the 2000 and 2004 presidential election that violated the Voting Rights Act.

There are disturbing similarities between the disenfranchisement of blacks at the turn of the twentieth and twenty-first centuries. A comparison of The Commission's studies on the progress of the Voting Rights Act in the 1960s and 1980s and recent elections reveal similar voting problems in the 2000 and 2004 presidential elections. The studies in 1960 and 1980 found obstacles to the enfranchisement of African Americans at polling sites. In some states, white election officials told blacks they could not find their names on the lists and were uncooperative and hostile when checking identity of the registration of blacks. Absentee ballots presented

Table 4.2 Common Voting Irregularities in the 2000 and 2004 Presidential
         Elections

Standards	Procedure	Practices
Lack of uniformity in voting systems in each county.	Voting machines with varying ballot rejection rates. Inadequate resources for voter education on how to use machines.	Faulty voting equipment. Voting machines that work in some precincts but not in others which prevent some voters from voting.
Lack of consistent standards on eligible absentee ballot statewide.	Varying procedures to accept ballots	Voters denied ballots because records wrongfully indicated they were mailed absentee ballots. Absentee ballots requested but never received. Absentee ballot sent to voters who did not request them.
Lack of consistent standards on provisional ballots statewide.	Varying procedures to accept ballots.	Voters not being allowed to have another ballot to correct mistakes. Denial of registered voters to cast ballots, at a disproportionate rate, in areas with a large population of African and Haitian American voters.
Absence of clear federal guidance on voter registration database and identification procedures.	Varying requirements for identification.	Voters told they could not vote because they did not have the proper ID, when they did. Some voters are asked for ID and others are not, and some are asked for photo or two forms of ID.
Poorly maintained voter list.	Failure to process motor voter registration.	Voters with voter registration cards and proper ID were not placed on the voter list and turned away.
Poorly designed purge list.	Erroneously purged a disproportionate number of minority voters.	Some voters were incorrectly turned away at the polls.

(Continued)

Table 4.2 Continued

Standards	Procedure	Practices
Lack of consistent polling place standards.	Inconsistent procedures for voter notification in each precinct about vital information regarding their polling sites.	Polling places closed early or moved without notice. In some precincts notification is not given to voters about polling place changes. Filthy conditions at some polling sites.
Inadequately trained poll workers.	Poll workers provided misinformation to voters or were unable to assist voters.	Poll workers neglected to use affidavits (provisional ballots) under appropriate conditions. Poll workers were unable to operate voting machines and assisted some voters by voting for them.
Failure to accommodate the disabled and language minorities.	Limited or no assistance at the polls.	Voters denied language assistance. Disabled denied access to polling booth.
Failure to accommodate a high voter turnout.	Insufficient amount of voting machines. Insufficient amount of ballots.	Long lines and poor conditions of the facilities led some people not to vote.

Source: Compiled by Percy (2004).

another set of problems with blacks receiving them late or not at all.[45] Similar voting problems for minorities in 2000 and 2004 elections demonstrate the Voting Rights Act has not eliminated disenfranchisement in America.

Studies have found that part of the problem with the protection of the Voting Right Act of 1965 signed by President Johnson is Section 5 of the Act. It targets certain states and local jurisdictions with an extensive practice of disenfranchisement.[46] These states are considered "covered" which means they should not implement any new election procedures without obtaining approval either by a three-judge United States District Court or by the Attorney General. But some of these covered jurisdictions do not comply with the requirements of the Act and have found various ways for noncompliance of the law. A study by the Southern Regional Council showed in just three states (Alabama, Georgia and South Carolina) there were 536 election law changes that were "enforced [in the state] but not submitted for preclearance under Section 5."[47] As these studies revealed the existence of noncompliance to the Act, the claims of the 2000 and 2004 election should have been given more urgent consideration by political leaders. In the 2000 presidential election, the executive, legislative, and judicial branches were unresponsive to voters' claims about irregularities.

> The real significance of the aftermath of the 2000 presidential election is the way that the disenfranchisement of blacks in Florida highlights the country's history of tolerating disenfranchisement across the board. Florida simply made visible an ongoing pattern of disenfranchisement within a larger pattern of exclusions based on race, class, and gender.[48]

Voting irregularities were perhaps the most important challenges in the 2000 and 2004 presidential election crises because as Thomas Paine once said, "Voting is the right upon which all other rights depend." Voting irregularities diluted the vote in many precincts and conflict with fundamental principles of our democratic system of government. "Indeed, no right is more precious in a free country than that of having a choice in the election of those who make the laws under which we live."[49] This investigation confirms that some voters in certain jurisdictions, and in particular African Americans, were disproportionately denied their most basic constitutional right to vote in the 2008 presidential primaries, and the 2004 and 2000 presidential elections.

Chapter 5

An Electoral System in Dispute: Harmful Rise in Election Lawsuits

Scarcely any political question arises in the United States that is not resolved sooner or later into a judicial question.

Alexis de Tocqueville

There is an unprecedented amount of election disputes in this country. The 2000 election debacle established a destructive trend to resolve election disputes—lawsuits. "The average number of cases in the 1996 to 1999 period was 96 per year, compared with an average of 254 cases per year from 2001 to 2004," and the numbers have sharply increased between the 2004 to 2008 period.[1]

These incessant amounts of election cases harm the electoral system in several ways. One, election lawsuits often raise barriers against legitimate voters because they often result in more election laws. Two, election laws and procedures are increasing rather than decreasing the complexities of the voting process. Three, increased election challenges reduce voter confidence and lead to the cycle of additional disputes before the courts.

The growing number of election lawsuits among candidates, political parties, voting and civil rights organizations, local election officials, and voters increased in every election this decade. Election lawsuits challenge a range of problems including electronic voting technology, electronic machine certification, voter photo identification, voter registration, proof of citizenship, paper trails for electronic machines, polling place challenges, provisional and absentee ballots, voting machine access for the disabled, and voters against electronic machine manufacturers. An assessment of these cases will demonstrate the divisive issues in our election process that have crippled our electoral system. A closer look at these cases will also show the confusion, complexities, and partisanship in the election processes, which are inconsistent with free elections in a democracy. These hotly contested cases weigh down our judicial system. But more important, these cases should signal the urgent need for reform measures to fix our broken system.

VOTING TECHNOLOGY

The most contentious aspect of the election process is the voting technology. The 2000 and 2004 presidential elections were plagued with voting technology problems that led to various lawsuits. There was also a vast amount of lawsuits preceding the 2008 presidential election. More than half the cases leading up to the 2008 election focused on the reliability and security of electronic voting systems. The most critical cases ranged from attempts to ban electronic machines to challenges of the manufacturers of electronic machines and state officials' certification of their use in the state.

Cases to Ban Electronic Voting Machines

In a recent drastic step to block the use of electronic machines nationwide, all fifty states have been sued in the National Clean Elections Lawsuit. The lawsuit is spearheaded by the We the People Foundation for Constitutional Education, with plaintiffs in every state.[2] In November 2007, the Foundation pledged that all secretaries of state in all fifty states would each receive subpoenas in the National Clean Elections Lawsuit, challenging the use of computerized vote counting machines. In the following public statement the Foundation described the intent of this federal voting rights case:

> Plaintiffs from every state brought the suit in the United States District Court for the Northern District of New York and maintain that current election practices, including the widespread use of computerized voting machines, are unconstitutional because they are ripe for fraud and error and effectively hide the physical vote counting process from the public, effectively denying citizens their legally protected Right to cast an effective vote.[3]

The lawsuit also seeks an Order from the Court to force election officials to use paper ballots. The Foundation stated it expects the case to go to the Supreme Court to ensure the integrity of elections. Other lawsuits, separate from the National Clean Elections Lawsuit, were filed in state courts in Arizona, California, New York, Florida, Pennsylvania, and Maryland and tried to bar those states' use of electronic voting machines.

Cases on the Reliability and Security of Electronic Machines

The state most embroiled in election lawsuits is Ohio. The cases challenge a range of election problems in Ohio, but most of the cases involve voting technology. The 2004 Ohio presidential election had similar voting problems as the 2000 Florida presidential election. Like Florida, the race in Ohio was close, there were long lines, inadequate poll worker training, and more important some of the voting machines did not capture the votes. Ohio has since scrapped the voting technology it used in the 2004 election. However, Ohio's recent efforts to upgrade its voting technology and election procedures have only led to several election lawsuits.

In January 2008, civil rights organizations filed the most recent case, *ACLU v. Brunner* to challenge the optical scan centralized system that Cuyahoga County planned to use to replace electronic machines.[4] In 2007, the county dropped the use of electronic machines after its study showed that the machines could be manipulated. The county had spent about $31 million to purchase electronic machines to replace the faulty punchcard system of the 2004 election. The county then determined it would use the optical scan centralized system that would send paper ballots to be scanned and counted at a central location. The optical scan system is permitted under the 2002 Help America Vote Act. One of the best features of this voting technology is that the voter inserts the ballot directly into the machine that can reject an overvote ballot or ballots that cannot be read. The voter therefore has the opportunity to correct the error before leaving the polls. This error feature significantly reduces the risk that an individual's vote will be rejected. However, Cuyahoga County did not purchase a voting system with the error notification feature, which led to the several current lawsuits.

The ACLU filed the current lawsuit *ACLU v. Brunner* because it said that with more than one million registered voters in Cuyahoga County for the 2008 election, the optical scan system does not give voters notice of ballot errors and an opportunity to correct mistakes that could invalidate their votes. They argue these machines provide "unequal, inaccurate and inadequate voting technology in Ohio's most populous county" and therefore do not improve the voting process.[5] The claim stated the optical scan centralized system violates the Fourteenth Amendment and the Voting Rights Act. They tried to block Cuyahoga County from using the new voting system. Meredith Bell-Platts, a staff attorney with the ACLU Voting Rights Project said, "Many votes will go uncounted if voters cannot verify that their ballots have been filled out correctly."[6]

In a similar 2006 ACLU case in Ohio, *Stewart v. Blackwell* challenged punch-card and central-count optical scan machines that did not provide voters with notification of ballot problems. "It is unacceptable for some Ohio voters to have the opportunity to identify and fix errors on their ballots, while other voters do not," said Carrie Davis, staff attorney for the ACLU.[7] The Court found that the state's use of punch-card ballots in some counties and electronic machines in other counties violated the Voting Rights Act as well as Ohio voters' equal protection and due process rights.[8]

Other electronic voting machine cases are being litigated simultaneously in state courts across the nation. Table 5.1 identifies the major voting technology cases, and the states in which voting systems are being challenged.

Table 5.1 Major Voting Technology Cases

Case	Issue	State
National Clean Elections Lawsuit	Ban electronic vote counting technology	All 50 states
ACLU of Ohio v. Brunner	Voting technology	Ohio
Ohio Democratic Party v. Blackwell	Voting technology	Ohio
Stewart v. Blackwell	Voting technology	Ohio
Callen v. Blackwell	Voting technology	Ohio
Banfield v. Courtes	Voting technology	Pennsylvania
Taylor v. Onorato	Voting technology	Pennsylvania
Fedder v. Gallagher	Voting technology	Florida
Wexler v. Lepore	Voting technology	Florida
Sarasota Alliance for Fair Elections v. Browning	Voting technology	Florida
United States of America v. New York Board of Elections	Voting technology	New York
Jennings v. Elections Canvassing Committee of Florida/Jennings v. Dent	Voting machine malfunction	New York
Holder v. McPherson	Ban electronic machines	California
San Diego County v. Bowen	Voting technology	California
Chavez v. Brewer	Ban electronic machines	Arizona

Source: Compiled by Percy (2008).

Electronic Machine Certification Cases

Voters in various states have sued their counties regarding the certification and utilization of electronic machines. They challenge the proper election administration of local officials to certify unreliable and insecure machines. For example, the North Carolina case *Joyce McCloy v. The North Carolina State Board of Elections* challenged North Carolina's certification of Diebold's electronic voting machines. The 2005 claim stated that North Carolina law requires the Board of Elections to thoroughly evaluate all voting systems. It argued the Board of Elections did not investigate the reliability and security of the electronic machines before it certified them. The plaintiffs claimed the law requires only safe and secure machines to gain certification, and therefore the electronic machines should be decertified. It asked the Court to grant a temporary restraining order to prohibit North Carolina's one hundred counties from buying any of the certified voting machines until the Board of Elections conducted a thorough assessment. It also said the Board did not meet its statutory obligations. In a separate lawsuit Diebold tried to skirt state election transparency laws. In *Diebold v. North Carolina Board of Elections,* the manufacturer claimed it could not comply with the "code escrow requirement of the state statute."[9]

Voters in other states also challenge the state certification of electronic machines. In *Linda Schade et al v. Maryland State Board of Elections and Linda Lamone,* Maryland voters sued the state to decertify Diebold electronic machines until it met security standards. The suit claimed the certification violated state and federal law, including Maryland Code, Election Law §§ 9-102 & 9-103. It cited specific provisions of Maryland law that stipulates the state board of elections *"may not certify"* a voting system unless the board determines the machines can "protect the security of the voting process . . . count and record all votes accurately and . . . be capable of creating a paper record of all votes cast in order that an audit trail is available in the event of a recount."[10]

Across the nation voters, political parties, and civil rights and voting rights organizations have challenged the proper election administration of local officials that certified unreliable and insecure voting machines. Table 5.2 identifies the major cases that challenged the certification of electronic machines.

Cases against Electronic Machine Manufacturers

Voters have brought lawsuits against electronic machine manufacturers for a variety of reasons. For example, in the landmark case *Online Policy Group v. Diebold,* the Internet Service Provider Online Policy Group, and two students, sued Diebold for attempting to infringe on their First Amendment rights.[11] This case involved the actions of Diebold that sent

Table 5.2 Cases on Improper Certification of Electronic Voting Machines

Case	Issue	State
King Lincoln Bronzeville Neighborhood association v. Blackwell	Improper election administration	Ohio
League of Women Voters of Florida v. Blackwell	Improper election administration	Ohio
Ohio Democratic Party v. Blackwell	Improper election administration	Ohio
In Re: Removal from Office of Members of the Cuyahoga County Board of Elections/Bennett v. Brunner	Improper election administration	Ohio
United States of America v. Brown	Improper election administration	Mississippi
Borders v. King County	Improper election administration	Washington
Commonwealth of Kentucky, Office of the Attorney General v. Commonwealth of Kentucky, State Board of Elections	Improper election administration	Kentucky
Monk v. Democratic National Committee	Improper election administration	Florida
Joyce McCloy v. The North Carolina State Board of Elections and the North Carolina Office of Information Technology Services	Improper election administration	North Carolina

Source: Compiled by Percy (2008).

numerous cease-and-desist letters to Internet Service Providers for hosting online their leaked internal documents that revealed security and reliability flaws in their electronic machines. The manufacturer claimed this was a copyright violation and used the Digital Millennium Copyright Act to demand that the documents be taken down from sites. The Online Policy Group challenged Diebold's copyright claims as an infringement on free speech that would prevent public debate about their voting machines. Judge Jeremy Fogel wrote, "No reasonable copyright holder could have believed that the portions of the email archive discussing possible technical problems with Diebold's voting machines were protected by copyright."[12] The court said Diebold abused the copyright claims of the Digital Millennium Copyright Act, which states it is illegal to use the Act to threaten "when the copyright holder knows that infringement has not actually occurred."[13] Diebold was found guilty of abusive copyright claims that led to subsequent damages and fees of $125,000.

In another case against a manufacturer, San Francisco sued Elections Systems & Software (ES&S) in 2007. In *San Francisco v. Election Systems & Software*, the City claimed ES&S did not provide the city with the most current version of the voting technology. It argued the company therefore breached its contract. The suit claimed the voting equipment did not meet state standards and the company needed to reimburse the City for related costs. This case was later settled.

In California, in *March v. Diebold*, voters filed a claim to prevent Diebold from installing voting systems that were uncertified. It used the RABA study conducted for Maryland's Diebold system, that indicated reliability and security flaws with electronic machines, to demonstrate that California's secretary of state should require security safeguards from the Diebold manufacturer. The temporary restraining order was denied by the judge.

Similar lawsuits against voting machine manufacturers also occurred after the 2000 presidential election. Voters sued the manufacturers of punch-card systems. One such case was *Wirth v. Election Systems and Software* (ES&S).[14] Voters who lived in counties that used the punch-card system filed the claim against the manufacturer, ES&S, for designing, manufacturing, advertising, and marketing the faulty system to their county. The plaintiffs argued the punch-card system was inferior and the company deliberately sold fraudulent products to various counties nationwide. They maintained the company violated the Equal Protection and Due Process Clauses because they are "state actors" performing a government function. Table 5.3 shows recent cases against voting machine manufacturers.

Disabled Persons' Access Cases

Voters with disabilities have sued in several states about their voting rights regarding voting technology. They challenge the state's electronic machines that fail to provide access for disabled voters. Disabled rights advocates and several disabled voters have filed lawsuits in state courts in Arizona, Florida, Colorado, and California.

Table 5.3 Suits Against Voting Technology Manufacturers

Case	Company	State
San Francisco v. Election System & Software Inc.	Diebold	California
Online Policy Group v. Diebold	ES&S	Not state specific
March v. Diebold	Diebold	Maryland
Wirth v. Election Systems and Software Inc.	ES&S	Florida

Source: Compiled by Percy (2008).

There have been numerous disability cases in California. In *American Association of People with Disabilities v. Secretary of State Kevin Shelly*, the plaintiffs claimed the Americans with Disabilities Act and state laws require voting machines to be accessible. It claimed that provisions of the California Elections Code violated those laws when it gave counties the directive to follow voting accessibility requirements when funds were available. In another California case, *Holder v. McPherson*, voters claimed that the security vulnerabilities of Diebold TSx violate state certification requirements and fail to provide access for disabled voters. The 2006 claim stated the denial of access for disabled voters violated the American with Disabilities Act.[15]

The 2004 disability case, *Peter Benavidez (Riverside County) et al. v. Secretary of State Kevin Shelley* was in sharp contrast to the other disputes in California. Disability voters wanted to reclaim the use of the electronic voting machines. They challenged California's switch from electronic voting machines, which they claim are accessible to disabled voters.[16] The claim said the State violated federal and state laws that affected disabled voters. The lawsuit was settled after a preliminary ruling against the plaintiff. In a similar 2005 case in Florida, disabled voters in *National Federation of the Blind v. Volusia County* tried to force Volusia County to use paperless e-voting machines. They argued it benefited disabled voters because the technology was accessible and easier to use.[17] In another case in Florida, the *American Association of People with Disability v. Hood*, disabled voters sued to order Duval County, Florida, to make voting accessible to voters.

Other disability cases in Arizona and Colorado attempt to ban the use of electronic voting systems. In Arizona, *Chavez v. Brewer* voters tried to bar electronic machines because they claimed the machines did not provide the disabled access and "present unacceptable risks of inaccuracy, vote manipulation, and malfunction."[18] The complaint also stated the machines did not meet state requirements. The Colorado case, *Conroy v. Dennis*, makes similar disability access claims.[19] Table 5.4 identifies the major cases that challenge disabled persons' ability to access electronic voting machines.

The number of voting technology cases to protect voting rights is growing in several states. Voting technology cases are viewed by activists as protecting the rights of every voter. These dramatic increases of cases in recent years are a result of the crippled electoral system.

VOTER IDENTIFICATION CASES

The second most contentious area in the election process is voter identification at polling places on Election Day. Voter identification cases are the first major election disputes to reach the U.S. Supreme Court, since the 2000 *Bush v. Gore* case. There are two main issues in the voter identification

Table 5.4 Disabled Persons' Access to Voting Machines Challenges

Case	Issue	State
American Association of People with Disability v. Hood	Disability access	Florida
National Federation of the Blind v. Volusia County	Disability access	Florida
Peter Benavidez (Riverside County) et al. v. Secretary of State Kevin Shelley	Disability access	California
American Association of People with Disabilities v. Secretary of State Kevin Shelly	Disability access	California
Holder v. McPherson	Disability access	California
Conroy v. Dennis	Disability access	Colorado
Chavez v. Brewer	Disability access	Arizona

Source: Compiled by Percy (2008).

(ID) dispute. The first problem is that some states enacted new laws that require voters' registration information to match with state and federal databases to be able to vote. The other issue is the new photo ID requirement in many states to be eligible to vote.

These two new election statutes have led to tumultuous election conflict and vast lawsuits, especially the photo ID requirement. Currently, seven states require voters to show a photo ID document, according to the National Conference of State Legislatures. About seventeen other states also require identification, but not photo IDs. One of the strictest photo ID laws in the country can be found in the state of Indiana; far stricter than the standards set out in the Help America Vote Act of 2002. In July 2005, Indiana adopted a state law that requires voters to have a current government issued photo ID to be able to cast a ballot. The law also requires voters without IDs to file a provisional ballot and in ten days provide a government-issued photo ID or file an affidavit that they are too poor to afford a government issued photo ID.

Two separate lawsuits were filed in the U.S. District Court for the Southern District of Indiana challenging the new voter photo ID requirements.[20] The two cases, *Crawford v. Marion County Election Board*, and *Indiana Democratic Party v. Rokita*, were heard together.[21] The plaintiffs claimed the Indiana law violated the First and Fourteenth Amendment and would disenfranchise poor, elderly, and minority voters. The plaintiffs argued Indiana stated it enacted the laws to prevent voter fraud but did not show any evidence in which a photo ID requirement would prevent voter fraud. The claim maintained evidence shows there is more voter fraud with absentee ballots, and the new law did not apply the restrictions to absentee ballots.

The 2007 decision by the Indiana court to uphold the state law was viewed as an extremely partisan opinion. The majority opinion was made by Republican judges, and the Democratic dissenting judge, Judge Terence T. Evans said, "Let's not beat around the bush: The Indiana voter photo ID law is a not-too-thinly-veiled attempt to discourage election-day turnout by certain folks believed to skew Democratic."[22] A *New York Times* article editorialized that all of the laws "have been pushed by Republican legislators who maintain that the laws are necessary to deter voter fraud. The laws have been resisted and challenged by Democrats who argue that they exaggerate the dangers and incidence of voter fraud while impermissibly sacrificing voter access."[23]

On January 9, 2008, the U.S. Supreme Court agreed to hear the Indiana Voter ID case *Crawford v. Marion County Election Board.* The question presented was: Whether the Indiana statute mandating that those seeking to vote in person produce government-issued photo ID violates the First and Fourteenth Amendments to the U.S. Constitution? The Supreme Court's verdict on April 28, 2008, ruled in favor of the Indiana law. The Court gives states the authority to require voters to produce photo ID. In the 6 to 3 decision, the Court said the law was necessary to prevent fraud, although there are no reports of such cases of fraud.

In another photo ID case, Georgia's Republican legislature passed a voter ID law that required voters to use a current government-issued photo ID card at the polls. Civil rights organizations challenged the law, and a federal judge invalidated the Georgia law. But the Georgia legislature passed a new version of the ID law. The voter ID law was again struck down by a federal judge as discriminatory. Judge Melvin Westmoreland of Fulton County Superior Court found the requirement violated the State Constitution because it placed "undue and unnecessary burdens on the fundamental right to vote."[24] The federal judge likened the restrictive regulation to a modern-day poll tax that prevents voters without passports, jobs, and drivers license from voting. Similarly in Missouri, the court invalidated a state law in 2006 for photo ID requirements.

In Wisconsin, the State legislature passed a constitutional amendment that required voter photo ID. The Wisconsin 2004 presidential election was plagued with election problems in Milwaukee, and the constitutional amendment, according to legislatures, aimed at resolving some of those election problems. The governor vetoed the amendment three times because he found it disenfranchised voters, especially the elderly and disabled, who do not have photo ID.[25]

The 2008 Indiana photo ID decision by the U.S. Supreme Court will help to settle these varying state requirements. The controversial Indiana case will influence election laws nationwide and, more important, influence the national election.

"Matching" Voter Identification Cases

Voter ID lawsuits challenge either photo ID or the "matching system." The new "matching system" is a new form of voter eligibility in which voters' information at the Department of Motor Vehicles must "match" with state and federal databases. This new election law in several states has led to many lawsuits.

The first lawsuit in the United States to invalidate the new procedure to "match" voter information from one database to another was the 2007 case *Washington Association of Churches v. Reed*. A coalition of voters challenged the Washington State law that would have barred citizens from voting unless the secretary of state could perfectly match their names, drivers' license, Social Security numbers, and birth dates on their voter registration forms, with other state and federal government databases.[26] The suit argued HAVA required each state to create a statewide database of registered voters but did not require the "matching" system adopted by the state of Washington. The plaintiffs claimed that if there was a matching error between the registration forms and the government records, that failure was not due to voter eligibility. Matching errors could result from computer glitches or human error that misspelt the names of women with hyphenated last names or individuals with foreign names.[27] The suit argued many eligible citizens were blocked from registering because of the "no match, no vote" rule.

Another recent voter ID case that involves "matching" is *Florida NAACP v. Browning*, filed in the U.S. District Court for the Northern District of Florida on September 17, 2007.[28] It challenged the state law that citizen's information must match the registration information in the new statewide voter database, and the motor vehicle and social security systems to be able to vote. Activists argue "the practice has already unduly delayed or denied the registration of more than 76,000 Florida citizens, with more than 14,000 still blocked from the rolls, and could disenfranchise far more in 2008 if not struck down."[29] The plaintiffs argued that human error in the state's database could lead to undue burdens that disfranchise eligible voters. On December 18, 2007, a federal judge forbade the Florida law. This case was appealed in the Eleventh Circuit Court of Appeals with arguments scheduled for 2008. Table 5.5 identifies the full extent to which voter ID is being challenged nationwide.

VOTER REGISTRATION CASES

Voter registration in the 2000 and 2004 presidential election was one of the most problematic areas of the elections. Voter registration continues to

Table 5.5 Voter Identification Cases

Case	Issue	State
ACLU of New Mexico v. Chavez	Photo voter ID	New Mexico
Common Cause, Georgia v. Billups	Photo voter ID	Georgia
Lake v. Perdue	Photo voter ID	Georgia
Crawford v. Marion County Election Board	Photo voter ID	Indiana
Indiana Democratic Party v. Rokita	Photo voter ID	Indiana
Navajo Nation v. Brewer	Voter ID	Arizona
Gonzalez v. Arizona	Voter ID	Arizona
Purcell v. Gonzalez	Voter ID	Arizona
NEOCH v. Blackwell	Voter ID	Ohio
American Civil Liberties of Minnesota v. Mary Kiffmeyer	Voter ID	Minnesota
In Re Request for Advisory Opinion Regarding Constitutionality of 2005 PA 71	Photo voter ID	Michigan
Jackson County v. State of Missouri Weinschenk v. State of Missouri	Photo voter ID	Missouri
NAACP v. Carnahan	Photo voter ID	Missouri
Washington Association of Churches v. Reed	Voter ID	Washington
Florida NAACP v. Browning	Voter ID	Florida

Source: Compiled by Percy (2008).

be a litigious aspect of the election process, which is demonstrated in the increasing amount of cases challenging the process. The improper purging of names from the voter rolls, missing voter eligibility information, lack of statewide databases for verification, and misspelt names of voters on the registration list have led to many lawsuits to settle the disputes.

In Ohio, civic organizations filed *Project Vote v. Blackwell* to challenge new voter registration provisions.[30] The plaintiffs claimed the new laws restricted the voter registration efforts by organizations. They argued against the strict rules and procedures in the statute and noted the following in their claim to the court:

> In the past, citizens working to register voters were able to turn in the completed forms to a civic group or church that would review the forms for accuracy, turn them into the registrar, and follow up later to make sure the voter was actually registered. Now, workers collecting voter registration forms would be forbidden from doing that and

would be subject to felony charges if the forms were to be handed in late or not directly to the registrars' offices.[31]

The lawsuit claimed the registration statutes violated the Voting Rights Act of 1965, the National Voter Registration Act of 1993, and the First and Fourteenth Amendments of the U.S. Constitution. A federal court in Cleveland blocked enforcement of the state law. There were similar cases in other counties in Ohio.

In Florida, *League of Women Voters of Florida v. Cobb* claimed voter registration groups were unconstitutionally restricted in their registration drive efforts by new Florida statutes.[32] The 2006 lawsuit stated the new laws placed limits on the handling of absentee ballots by third parties. The plaintiffs challenged the Florida law that gave third-party registration groups a shorter deadline to return forms and imposed heavy fines for errors.[33] They argued the new law did not apply to political parties, which was discriminatory against voter registration groups. A federal district court blocked the enforcement of the new Florida law. There were similar voter registration cases in the state as well as other states such as Michigan, Pennsylvania, Washington, Alabama, Maryland, and Louisiana.

Proof of Citizenship Cases

Another significant problem in voter registration and at the polls is the proof of citizen requirement in some states. Illegal immigration became a major political issue after the September 11, 2001, terrorist attacks. Many states developed new policies and procedures to help deter illegal immigration. One such strategy was to enact election laws to keep illegal immigrants out of the political process. But the restrictions have led to numerous lawsuits.

In Arizona the case *Gonzalez v. Arizona* challenged Proposition 200 that required voters to present proof of citizenship as a condition for voter registration.[34] The 2006 case argued that in Arizona's effort to prevent illegal immigrants from voting, it imposed proof of citizenship burdens on thousands of citizens. The plaintiff claimed that millions of Americans rarely have readily available documentation that proves citizenship. The claim stated the Arizona law, Proposition 200, would rarely affect illegal immigrants who often did not try to vote but would instead deter eligible voters.

In 2006, the voter ID law in Arizona went before the U.S. Supreme Court in *Purcell v. Gonzalez*. The U.S. Supreme Court ruled states could actually disenfranchise voters with these laws. The Supreme Court said, "Voter fraud drives honest citizens out of the democratic process and breeds distrust of our government. Voters who fear their legitimate votes would be outweighed by fraudulent ones would feel disenfranchised."[35]

In a similar case in Ohio, *Boustani v. Blackwell* challenged the state law that allowed poll workers to require proof of naturalized citizenship. Voters who could not prove citizenship could cast a provisional ballot and provide proof in ten days at the Board of Elections. If they could not locate their document they could pay $200 for new copies, which could take up to a year. This denied the right of eligible voters from voting in the election in which they cast the provisional ballot. The state law did not require similar proof of citizenship from voters who claimed to be born in the United States. Therefore, the suit argued the statute violated the constitution by discriminating against one set of U.S. citizens to cast their ballot. Furthermore, the plaintiffs argued voting requirements based on the place of birth could lead to ethnic and racial profiling that would discourage minority groups from voting. The plaintiffs explained the statute violated the Constitution in the following manner:

> The law violated the First and Fourteenth Amendments, the Civil Rights Act of 1964, because only naturalized citizens needed to show proof of citizenship and because such proof was not necessary to determine an individual's eligibility status; and constituted a poll tax on naturalized citizens, in violation of the Twenty-Fourth and Fourteenth Amendments because individuals who need to replace or modify their naturalization papers must pay more than $200 to obtain a replacement certificate.[36]

In 2006, the court found the statute was unconstitutional for imposing undue burdens on the right to vote and violated the Fourteenth Amendment. Table 5.6 identifies the major voter registration cases in recent years.

POLLING PLACE CHALLENGES

There have been various problems at the polls in recent elections. Many jurisdictions had inadequately trained poll workers, insufficient machines, long lines, polling sites moved without voter notification, and reports of voter intimidation and discrimination. These problems were brought to the forefront in the 2000 presidential election at three public hearings, yet similar problems persisted in the 2004 presidential election. Voters have sued in several states about the various polling place challenges. The media has also sued about access that is being denied to the press to conduct exit polls. Table 5.7 identifies these major cases about election problems at the polls.

PROVISIONAL AND ABSENTEE BALLOTS

The 2004 presidential election survey sponsored by the federal Election Assistance Commission and conducted by the Election Data Services found

Table 5.6 Voter Registration Cases

Case	Issue	State
Diaz v. Hood	Voter registration	Florida
League of Women Voters of Florida v. Cobb	Voter registration	Florida
Harkless v. Blackwell	Voter registration	Ohio
Boustani v. Blackwell	Voter registration	Ohio
Citizens Alliance for Secure Elections v. Vu	Voter registration	Ohio
Project Vote v. Blackwell	Voter registration	Ohio
Lucas County Democratic Party v. Blackwell	Voter registration	Ohio
Miller v. Blackwell	Voter eligibility	Ohio
United States v. Alabama	State voter registration databases	Alabama
Acorn v. Dickerson	Voter registration	Maryland
Grebner v. Michigan	State voter registration databases	Michigan
Purcell v. Gonzalez	Voter proof of citizenship	Arizona
Gonzalez v. Arizona	Voter proof of citizenship	Arizona
Segue v. Louisiana	Voter registration	Louisiana
Service Employees International Union Local #3 v. Municipalities of Monroeville and Lebanon	Voter registration	Pennsylvania

Source: Compiled by Percy (2008).

that at least 1.9 million voters cast provisional ballots nationwide in 2004. However, these ballots were not all counted according to different rules in various states. The study found that about 26 percent of absentee ballots, including military and overseas voters, were disqualified for procedural reasons, depending on the jurisdiction to which the ballots were mailed. The disparate treatment of provisional and absentee ballots led to numerous lawsuits in several states.

The state of Ohio received the most lawsuits. In the 2004 presidential election, an unprecedented amount of voters in Ohio cast provisional ballots. Approximately 22 percent of the 157,714 provisional ballots cast in the state were not counted (nearly thirty-four thousand ballots).[37] There are several lawsuits challenging the rejection of many of those ballots.

Table 5.7 Polling Place Challenges

Case	Issue	State
Democratic National Committee v. Republican National Committee	Polling place challenges	New Jersey
Florida Democratic Party v. Cobb	Polling place notices	Florida
CBS Broadcasting v. Cobb	Polling place, Press access	Florida
Ohio Democratic Party v. Blackwell	Polling place challenges	Ohio
Spencer v. Blackwell	Polling place challenges	Ohio
State of Ohio Ex Rel. Matthew Wolf v. Blackwell	Polling place challenges	Ohio
Summit County Democratic Central Executive Committee v. Blackwell	Polling place challenges	Ohio
American Broadcasting Companies v. Blackwell	Polling place, Press access	Ohio
Beacon Journal Publishing Company Inc. and Charlene Nevada v. Kenneth Blackwell and the Board of Elections	Polling place, Press access	Ohio
ABC, Inc. v. Heller	Polling place, Press access	Nevada

Source: Compiled by Percy (2008).

In the 2006 lawsuit *State of Ohio and The People for the American Way Foundation v. Kenneth Blackwell and the Cuyahoga County Board of Elections* voters asserted the state had inadequate guidance for counting provisional ballots and lacked uniform standards. The complaint stated election officials and poll workers were given inconsistent and erroneous instruction about provisional ballots that led to confusion and disparate treatment of the ballots. The plaintiffs claimed that poll workers used erroneous electronic registration databases, instead of the registration cards filled out by voters, to determine if a provisional voter was eligible to vote. The complaint alleged the following:

> This was a violation of the Voting Rights Act, which prohibits the denial of the right to vote due to an "error or omission on any record or paper relating to any application, registration, or other act requisite to voting, if such error or omission is not material in determining whether such individual is eligible under State law to vote in such election."[38]

The suit claimed that provisional ballots were rejected because of minor errors such as a missing signature from a poll worker. This violates provisions of the Voting Rights Act. The suit also claimed the voters' rights, under the Equal Protection Clause, the Help America Vote Act, and the Due Process Clause were all denied in the rejection of provisional ballots. The plaintiffs wanted the court to prevent election officials from rejecting provisional ballots until they checked the paper registration records. It also asked the court to bar the rejection of registration forms without signature if the voter has signed elsewhere, and grant voters written notice if the county planned to reject their provisional ballots.

A similar 2004 Ohio case about provisional ballots was, *Schering v. Blackwell* in U.S. District Court.[39] The plaintiffs claimed the secretary of state did not provide Ohio's eighty-eight counties with specific and consistent directions for provisional ballots. It claimed this violated Ohio statutes,[40] and the Equal Protection Clause. There were cases in other states challenging the rejection of provisional and absentee ballot cases. Table 5.8 lists provisional and absentee ballot cases across the United States.

VOTER VERIFICATION PAPER TRAIL CASES

The recent studies on electronic machines that exposed flaws in the technology led to numerous lawsuits demanding paper trails and regular audits to help ensure the security of the ballot. Voter verification disputes are led mostly by activists rather than voters. There has been an historic proliferation of numerous nonprofit organizations established by activists to help demand voter-verified paper records nationwide. They have established Websites, conducted studies, published books, and used other significant tools to influence election officials to reform the electoral system. When these methods proved ineffective to bring about change, activists used lawsuits to pressure national and state legislators to use voter-verified paper records. For example, activists led the effort to sue all fifty states in the National Clean Elections lawsuit, challenging the use of electronic voting machines to record and count the vote without a paper trail. The lawsuit also tried to gain greater transparency in the counting of ballots in the 2008 presidential primary and general elections.

In another advocacy led case, *Soubirous v. County of Riverside*, a former political candidate from California who lost a 2004 race by forty-five votes, and the voter advocacy organization, VerifiedVoting.org, filed suit against the county registrar who would not grant access to the audit logs of electronic voting systems for verification of votes in the 2004 election. In another case, the ACLU in Florida filed the lawsuit *ACLU Florida v. Florida Department of State* to change a rule by the Department of State that denied manual recounts on electronic voting machines. The 2004 claim stated voting machines that denied manual recounts violated Florida Election Codes that required manual recounts in close elections.

Table 5.8 Provisional and Absentee Ballot Cases

Case	Issue	State
Meehan v. Philadelphia Board of Commissioners	Absentee ballots	Pennsylvania
Reitz et al v. The Honorable Edward G. Rendell et al	Absentee ballots	Pennsylvania
United States of America v. The Commonwealth of Pennsylvania et al	Absentee ballots	Pennsylvania
Landes v. Tartaglione	Absentee ballots	Pennsylvania
Ray v. State of Texas	Absentee ballots	Texas
AFL-CIO v. Hood	Provisional ballot	Florida
Florida Democratic Party v. Hood	Provisional ballot	Florida
Bay County Democratic Party v. Land	Provisional ballot	Michigan
Hawkins v. Blunt	Provisional ballot	Missouri
Colorado Common Cause v. Donetta Davidson	Provisional ballot	Ohio
Kilroy v. Franklin County Board of Elections	Provisional ballot	Ohio
League of Women Voters of Ohio v. Blackwell	Provisional ballot	Ohio
Sandusky County Democratic Party v. Kenneth Blackwell	Provisional ballot	Ohio
Sarah White v. Kenneth Blackwell and the Board of Elections of Lucas County, Ohio	Provisional ballot	Ohio
Schering v. Blackwell	Provisional ballot	Ohio
State of Ohio and The People for the American Way Foundation v. Kenneth Blackwell and the Cuyahoga County Board of Elections	Provisional ballot	Ohio
Washington State Democratic Central Committee v. King County Records, Elections and Licensing Services Division	Provisional ballot	Washington

Source: Compiled by Percy (2008).

Individual voters also challenge the use of electronic machines without paper trails. Litigations on verified voting from individual voters went before the court in Florida, California, North Carolina, Pennsylvania, Ohio, and Maryland. For example, in Maryland, voters challenged the adoption of electronic machines without the paper trail for voter verification *in Linda Schade et al v. Maryland State Board of Elections and Linda Lamone.* Another example is the Ohio case *White v. Blackwell* in which the voter Jeanne White asked the court to ensure verifiability of votes in Ohio. The case eventually went to federal court and asked the court to require Ohio to adopt election laws that would increase the security and audit capability of voting machines. The plaintiff stated the goal of the case was to impact election reform measures nationwide for uniform standards and processes.

In New Jersey, voters in the case of *Gusciora v. McGreevey* asked the court to ban the use of electronic machines until the state utilized the voter verifiable paper ballots.[41] The 2006 case argued the paperless electronic voting system deprived voters in the New Jersey their right to vote because the machines could not be used in a recount or an audit. State legislators passed a bill during the case that required all electronic machines in New Jersey to produce the voter-verifiable paper ballot by 2008. In another case about recount, one candidate claimed in *Wexler v. Lepore* that the use of electronic machines with no recount capabilities violated federal and state laws. The 2004 case also claimed there was unequal treatment of voters in fifteen Florida counties that could not conduct recount. These are other cases in other states challenging the lack of paper trail. Table 5.9 identifies the major cases asking courts to mandate a voter verification paper trail for electronic machines.

The unprecedented record of election lawsuits in the United States reinforces the need for election reform. But election reform is mired in partisan

Table 5.9 Voter Verification Cases

Case	Issue	State
Gusciora v. McGreevey	Mandate paper trail	New Jersey
Anita Rios v. Blackwell	Recount procedures	Ohio
Lopez Torres v. New York State Board of Elections	Ballot access	New York
Nader v. Blackwell	Ballot access	Ohio
National Clean Elections Lawsuit	Paper trail and ban system	All 50 states
Linda Schade et al v. Maryland State Board of Elections and Linda Lamone	Paper trail	Maryland
White v. Blackwell	Paper trail	Ohio
County of San Diego v. Bowen	Audit requirements	
Soubirous v. County of Riverside	Ballot access	
ACLU Florida v. Florida Department of State	Manual recount	Florida
Wexler v. Lepore	Recount	Florida

Source: Compiled by Percy (2008).

politics. Consequently, election disputes will continue to increase in future elections, because voters lack confidence in the process and are suing to protect their rights. Voting rights must be regarded as a nonpartisan election issue which has widespread impact on the national election results. Only a nonpartisan approach to election reform will help to reduce election lawsuits and improve confidence in the election process.

Chapter 6

Presidential Election Crisis: Who Should Resolve Another Presidential Election Dispute—The People or the Courts?

The Truth is, all men having power ought to be distrusted to a certain degree.

James Madison[1]

Our broken electoral system is, in part, a consequence of leaving the administration of national elections to state and local officials. A presidential election is an election for the entire nation, not a statewide office. "A few states with particularly flawed systems can hold the rest of the country hostage,"[2] similar to the 2000 presidential election debacle in Florida that went all the way to the U.S. Supreme Court.

As many Americans believe the controversial 2000 presidential election was decided by the Supreme Court, voters are concerned if they, the people, not the Court, will determine the president of United States in another disputed election.

There are still many unanswered question about the role the U.S. Supreme Court should play in a presidential election dispute. In deciding the 2000 presidential election outcome, was the U.S. Supreme Court designated by the Constitution as the final authority to resolve presidential election disputes? What was the early political thought of the U.S. founding fathers concerning separation of powers, federalism, and judicial independence? The framers included these fundamental democratic principles in the design of the American government to safeguard against abuse of power. We must understand these constitutional principles and the historical context of the Supreme Court in the American political system to clarify whether the U.S Supreme Court usurped its role in the 2000 presidential election dispute and should not have a similar role in a presidential election dispute.

FEDERALISM IN THE AMERICAN POLITICAL SYSTEM

The 2000 presidential election dispute raised important issues about federalism[3]—the authority of the U.S. Supreme Court in the case of *Bush v. Gore* to overturn a decision by the Florida Supreme Court that sought to clarify Florida election laws and procedures challenged by presidential candidate Al Gore.[4] The historic review below reveals the Supreme Court's role in the 2000 election conflicted with its own historical practices regarding judicial federalism, and the framers' overall intent of this democratic principle of state sovereignty.

Framers' Intent of Federalism

There was little debate on judicial federalism by the framers at the Constitution Convention. However, the framers' overall goal for federalism is clear; their primary concern was the safeguarding of liberties.[5] Justice Kennedy, in the concurring opinion in *United States v. Lopez*, 514 U.S 549 (1995), offered a similar explanation concerning the goal of federalism; "Though on the surface the idea may seem counterintuitive, [federalism] was the insight of the framers that freedom was enhanced by the creation of two governments, not one."[6]

The Constitution the framers enacted, with its democratic principles, established the basic structure of the federal court system. Today, the federal courts' power is derived from Article III of the Constitution, the Judiciary Act of 1789, and the Supremacy Clause. The federal courts' review of cases from the state courts is based on two criteria: one, cases from the state court must involve a federal matter; two, the Court will only review final decisions from the state's Supreme Court.[7] The jurisdiction and powers of the courts developed overtime, as there are no clear directives in historical records of the convention and ratification debates on the relationship between the two court systems. We are, therefore, left to rely on historical practices to determine the role of the two courts in the American system of government. As Alexander Hamilton summarized in Federalist Paper No. 82, "Time only can mature and perfect so compound a system, liquidate the meaning of all the parts, and adjust them to each other in a harmonium and consistent whole."[8]

Historical Practice of Judicial Federalism

Much of our understanding of federalism evolved through historical practices. Gradually after ratification, the role of the courts began to be defined in the new government. State courts began to directly challenge the powers of the federal courts. These cases that served to define the federal courts' power include: *Martin v. Hunter's Lessee*, 1 Wheaton 304 U.S. (1816), the Supreme Court established it may review state court decisions based on federal laws; *Chisholm v. Georgia*, 2 Dallas 419 (1793), the Court ruled against a state, which eventually led to the adoption of the Eleventh Amendment; *McCulloch v. Maryland*, 4 Wheaton 316 (1819), determined that states could not impose taxes on the bank established by the national government; *Gibbons v. Ogden*, 9 Wheaton 1 (1824), established that the federal government had the authority to regulate interstate commerce according to the commerce and the supremacy clauses.

In *Worchester v. Georgia*, 6 Peters 515 (1832), the Court's ruling had a different effect. It ordered the release of Samuel Worcester, who was being held for violating a state law that required whites to obtain a state license before residing on Cherokee land. The Georgia Supreme Court claimed the High Court did not have jurisdiction over state court decisions and refused to comply with the Court's order to release Worcester. This was the ruling in which President Jackson is said to have made the famous comment, "John Marshall has made this decision, and now let him enforce it."[9] This case illustrates the struggle of the Supreme Court to be respected as the final interpreter of the Constitution. After the Civil War the Court became very active in interpreting the Fourteenth Amendment. It struck down various state and national laws, which served to increase its powers and importance as the branch of government that protects the Constitution. The role of the Supreme Court to review decisions of the state courts and the other branches was further established in this period.

The Court further defined the relationship between the federal and state courts in *Murdock v. City of Memphis*, 87 U.S. 20 Wall (1875). The Court established that it would not review state decisions unless the state court's interpretation was ambiguous on the grounds to which it was based. This principle, which has come to define federalism in the court system, is called the "adequate and independent state grounds test." The rule maintains if a state's decision is based on adequate and independent state grounds, the Supreme Court will not review the case. In *Herb v. Pitcairn*, 324 U.S. 117 (1945) the Court more clearly explained this principle in the following statement:

> This Court from the time of its foundation has adhered to the principle that it will not review judgments of state courts that rest on adequate and independent state grounds. The reason . . . is found in the partitioning of power between the state and federal judicial systems and in the limitations of our own jurisdictions. Our only power over state judgments is to correct them to the extent that they incorrectly adjudge federal rights. And our power is to correct wrong judgments, not to revise opinions. We are not permitted to render an advisory opinion, and if the same judgments would be rendered by the state court after we corrected its views of federal laws, our review could amount to nothing more than an advisory opinion.[10]

The federal courts can review state court decisions when it's unclear whether the decision is based on state or federal law. However, the Court established in *Michigan v. Long* 463 U.S. 1032 (1983) that state court decisions could avoid review if a "plain statement" was included in the grounds of the decision. The Court explained, "If the state court decision indicates clearly and expressly that it is alternatively based on bona fide separate, adequate, and independent grounds, we, of course, will not undertake to review the decision."[11] The Court also established in the case the "plain statement" specifications:

> If a state court chooses merely to rely on federal precedents as it would on the precedent of all other jurisdictions, then it need only make clear by a plain statement in its judgment or opinion that the federal cases are being used only for the purpose of guidance and do not themselves compel the result that the court has reached.[12]

Michigan v. Long served to further define the relationship between the federal and state courts. The Court also stated the following:

> Respect for the independence of state courts, as well as avoidance of rendering advisory opinions, have been the cornerstones of the court's refusal to decide cases where there is an adequate and independent grounds. It is precisely because of this respect for state courts, and this desire to avoid advisory opinions, that we do not wish to continue to decide issues of state law that go beyond the opinion that we review,

or to require state courts to reconsider cases to clarify the grounds of their decisions.[13]

The adequate and independent state grounds doctrine was also recognized during the Burger Court era. Justice Brennan encouraged state courts during the Burger Court era to use state laws, not federal laws, to protect individual rights.[14] As Harold Spaeth explained, "The use of state constitutional provisions and statutory law for this purpose was unobjectionable ... because federal law sets a floor on rights, rather than a ceiling."[15]

Justices Brennan and Marshall, in their dissenting opinion in *Michigan v. Mosley*, 423 U.S. 102 (1975), also explained that state courts could use their constitutions and statutes to reach more liberal decisions, and under the adequate and independent doctrine the High Court would not hear the case. They also pointed out that in the lower federal courts, which had predominantly conservative justices appointed by Nixon, decisions grounded in state law could get around a review by these justices.[16] In an article in *Harvard Law Review*, Justice Brennan elaborated on this legal interpretation and application in more detail. He wrote:

> The essential point I am making ... is not that the United States Supreme Court is necessarily wrong in its interpretation of the federal Constitution ... it is simply that decisions of the Court are not, and should not be, dispositive of questions regarding rights guaranteed by counterpart provisions of state law. Accordingly, such decisions are not mechanically applicable to state law issues, and state court judges, and the members of the bar seriously err if they so treat them.[17]

In the modern court, Justices such as Sandra Day O'Connor acknowledged state autonomy in a speech, in which she stated, "A state determines whether to grant or withhold jurisdiction to the Supreme Court by the choice and articulation of the grounds for the state court decision."[18]

The increased application over the years of state courts' use of the adequate and independent grounds test in decisions led to what scholars are calling "new judicial federalism."[19] The term is used in three ways: to describe the relationship between the federal courts and state courts; to clarify the division of power or responsibility of the state courts; and to explain decisions of state courts based on state constitutions that protect individual rights so as to prevent federal court review of the cases.[20] A growing number of studies have examined the latter usage of the term, and the conclusions remain consistent with each other that generally the

Supreme Court does not review state court decisions based on state law. One of the most recent works on judicial federalism is by Michael Solimne and James Walker who noted the following:

> The present language of the statute permitting Supreme Court review of state court decisions, 28 U.S.C. §1257(a), seems to limit such review to issues arising under federal law. While the language of that provision and its predecessor statutes has not been informed by the text and history of Article III, it has been persuasively argued that rightly understood, there is no barrier derived from Article III that prevents the Supreme Court from reviewing even the state law decisions of state courts. The barrier is better viewed as a prudential one, based on respect for state autonomy when a state court interprets its own law.[21]

2000 Election Crisis and Federalism

Many legal scholars argue the Rehnquist majority's ruling in *Bush v. Gore* was inconsistent with the Court's traditional support of the adequate and independent grounds test. The Florida Supreme Court, in both election disputes it heard on the 2000 election crisis, relied on state law and therefore met the adequate and independent test. The Florida Supreme Court in *Palm Beach County Canvassing Board v. Harris*, 772 So. 2d 1220 (2000) stated in its ruling:

> Section 102.111, which provides that the Secretary "shall" ignore late returns, conflicts with section 102.112, which provides that the Secretary "may" ignore late returns. In the present case, we have used traditional rules of statutory construction to resolve these ambiguities to the extent necessary to address the issues presented here.[22]

Again in *Gore v. Harris*, 772 S.2d 1243 (2000) the Florida Supreme Court similarly based its opinion on Florida statutes. The court clearly stated the grounds of its decision:

> The Legislature of this State has placed the decision for election of President of the United States, as well as every other elected office, in the citizens of the State through a statutory scheme. These statutes established by the Legislature govern our decision today. We consider these statutes cognizant of the federal grant of authority derived from the United States Constitution and derived from 3 U.S.C.

§5 (1994) . . . This case today is controlled by the language set forth by the Legislature in section 102.168, Florida Statutes (2000).[23]

Justice Ginsburg in her dissent of *Bush v. Gore* discussed the long-established relationship and deference the Court has always granted state courts to interpret their own state laws. She cited several cases to show that historically the High Court did not review state court interpretation unless it conflicted with the Constitution. She identified cases when the Court disagreed with the interpretations but still deferred to the state courts, "unless it violated the expressed intent of Congress."[24] She asserted that in the Court's review of state law, the Court "dealt with such cases ever mindful of the full measure of respect we owe to interpretations of state law by a State's highest court."[25]

Justice Ginsburg argued that the Court has traditionally practiced what she called "cooperative judicial federalism." She discussed an example of a case that was litigated just one year before the 2000 election dispute, *Fiore v. White* (1999). In this case, instead of resolving the Pennsylvania state law dispute, the Supreme Court sent the issue to the Pennsylvania Supreme Court to "help determine the proper state-law predicate for our determination of the federal constitutional questions raised."[26] Even Chief Justice Rehnquist acknowledged in the concurrence, "In most cases, comity and respect for federalism compel us to defer to the decision of state courts on issues of state law. That practice reflects our understanding that the decisions of state courts are definitive pronouncements of the will of the States as sovereigns."[27] Although the Chief Justice cited three cases to demonstrate that the Court has not always followed this traditional course of federalism,[28] Justice Ginsburg argued the cases are probably the only three cases in the history of the Court that could be referred to as examples as well as they are incomparable to *Bush v. Gore*. Two of the three cases Rehnquist cited concerned the civil rights movement and the other case involved states' rights. Justice Ginsburg noted, "The Florida Supreme Court concluded that counting every legal vote was the overriding concern of the Florida Legislature when it enacted the State's Election Code. The court surely should not be bracketed with state high courts of the Jim Crow South."[29]

The Rehnquist majority, who defended federalism in the past, ignored years of precedent by "second-guessing" the Florida Supreme Court's interpretation of state law in the 2000 presidential election dispute.[30] The Court's acceptance of the case was inconsistent with judicial federalism. The Court's historic practice to defer to state courts on state law should have kept the case out of the jurisdiction of the High Court in the 2000 election and any similar future presidential election dispute.

SEPARATION OF POWERS IN THE AMERICAN POLITICAL SYSTEM

Constitutional debates over separation of powers during the 2000 election crisis involved whether Congress or the Supreme Court should serve as the final authority to resolve presidential election disputes. The Court has historically limited its power of judicial review in political matters. This self-imposed limitation is the political question doctrine that the Court has used to dismiss numerous cases that concerned political issues more properly addressed by another branch. The Court established guidelines in *Baker v. Carr* to distinguish matters with a political question. The historic review below shows *Bush v. Gore* met the guidelines the Court has used to determine political questions.

Framers' Intent of Separation of Powers

An examination of the separation of powers doctrine is critical to understanding the framers intent and assesses how the Court is limited in the structure of separation of powers. The concept of separation of powers existed long before it became a part of the U.S. Constitution.[31] The foundations of the separation of powers principle can be traced to the ancient Greek and Roman description of mixed government.[32] The works of these early writers greatly affected the framers' design of the Constitution.[33] For example, the framers cited the works of Locke and Montesquieu extensively in their discussions of the new government. Locke and Montesquieu built on the works of early theorists and are considered the foremost writers who influenced the separation of powers concept in America. John Locke's main contribution to the development of the separation of powers doctrine was the division of powers between two branches.[34] In his 1690 work *Civil Government*, Locke divided the functions of the executive and legislative branches into one to enact laws and the other to punish violaters of the law. Locke's two branches of government were later expanded by Montesquieu in the 1748 *Spirit of the Laws*.

Montesquieu's work expanded the theory of separation of powers.[35] His doctrine included a separate judiciary from the executive and legislative branches. His theories of separation of powers specified that individuals could not be members in more than one branch of government, and one branch could not usurp the authority of another branch. He explained that "there would be an end of everything, were the same men or the same body, whether of the nobles or of the people, to exercise those three powers, that of enacting laws, that of executing the public resolution, and of trying the causes of individuals."[36]

Montesquieu was concerned with the external influences on government and focused on protecting liberties. He concluded that the powers of government must be limited in order to protect individual rights.

> Political liberty is to be found only in moderate government, and even in these it is not always found. It is there only when there is no abuse of power. But constant experience shows us that every man invested with power is apt to abuse it. . . . To prevent this abuse it is necessary from the very nature of things that power should be a check to powers. A government should be so constituted, as no man shall be compelled to do things, which the law does not oblige him, nor forced to abstain from things, which the law permits.[37]

He believed an independent judiciary would also help to safeguard against tyranny. He acknowledged the importance of an independent judiciary to protect liberties when he wrote the following:

> There is no liberty if the judiciary power be not separate from the legislative and executive. Were it joined with the legislative, the life and liberty of the subject would be exposed, to arbitrary control; for the judge would then be the legislator. Were it joined to the executive power, the judge might behave with violence and oppression.[38]

The theories of the early political writers were refined by the framers of the U.S. Constitution.[39] Their goal during the founding was to safeguard liberties and citizens from tyranny.[40] Therefore, the framers instituted the separation of powers principles to limit the powers of government with no branch having authority over another. Madison argued the following:

> But the greatest security against a gradual concentration of the several powers in the same department, consists in giving to those who administer each department, the necessary constitutional means, and personal motives, to resist encroachments of the others.[41]

Madison also maintained that separation of powers was aimed at preventing any one class from controlling the decisions of society. He wrote that the "blending and balancing" of many classes were important to maitain a stable government. Madison, in the Federalist Paper No. 51 acknowledged the following:

> It is of great importance in a republic not only to guard against the oppression of its rulers, but to guard one part of the society against

the injustice of the other. Different interests necessarily exist in different classes of citizens. If a majority be united by a common interest the rights of the minority will be insecure.[42]

The framers strongly favored a new government with a *separation of powers*, although the term is not explicitly written in the Constitution. The first three articles of the Constitution establishes the democratic principle of separation of powers. It divides the three branches of government and specifies each branch's powers and limitations.[43] The question then becomes, how has the Court defined its powers and limitations so as not to usurp the role of another branch of government? An historical review sheds light on the Court's practices.

Historical Practice of Separation of Powers

The U.S. Supreme Court has defined and limited its powers based on Article III.[44] The Court's interpretation of Article III places three major constraints on its powers: "jurisdiction," "standing," and "justiciability."[45] These limitations have defined the High Court's responsibilities as well as the federal and lower courts' jurisdiction.

The constraint, "justiciability," is appropriate for our discussion because it means the case must be appropriate for resolution by the courts. Therefore, cases reviewed by the High Court must be justificiable—appropriate for the court to hear and give a decision.[46] The Court further defined the types of issues that would not meet "justiciability." If there are issues of "mootness, ripeness, standing, advisory opinions, and political questions" the case does not meet justiciability—so the court will not hear the case.[47]

Based on the justiciability political question doctrine the Court should have deferred the 2000 election dispute in the matter of *Bush v. Gore* to another branch of government. The political question doctrine holds that certain questions that are both constitutional and political will not be reviewed by the Court because they would be more appropriately addressed by another branch of government with clear responsibilities.[48] An historical review of political issues dismissed by the Court will demonstrate what exactly constitutes a political question.

The Court addressed the political question doctrine in *Luther v. Borden*, 7 Howard 1 (1849).[49] The case involved Rhode Island citizens who challenged the state legislature's property requirements for voting. The Court said Article IV did not grant the judiciary the authority to resolve the conflict. It claimed Congress or the president could more appropriately make a determination about the voting requirements. It ruled it would not address "political" questions. For more than one hundred years, the Court deferred political questions to another branch of government. In 1914, the Court in *Ohio ex rel. Davis V. Heldebrant*, 241 U.S. 565 (1916) dismissed state legislative apportionment challenges as nonjusticiability. Also, in the 1940s in *Colegrove v. Green*, 328 U.S. 549 (1946) Chief Justice Frankfurter rejected the case arguing that the political issue of legislative reapportionment "courts ought not to enter this political thicket."[50] Years later the Court would hear the reapportionment issue in the matter of *Baker v. Carr*, 369 U.S. 186 (1962). This case is significant to the development of the political question doctrine because the Court established guidelines to classify cases that are political questions, in which it will not review. It presented the following six guidelines:

> Prominent on the surface of any case held to involve a political question is found a textually demonstrable constitutional commitment of the issue to a coordinate political department; or a lack of judicially discoverable and manageable standards for resolving it; or the impossibility of deciding without an initial policy determination of a kind clearly for nonjudicial discretion; or the impossibility of a court's undertaking independent resolution without expressing lack of respect due coordinate branches of government; or an unusual need for unquestioning adherence to a political decision already made; or the potentiality of embarrassment from multifarious pronouncements by various departments of one question.[51]

There were several cases that followed *Baker v. Carr* that demonstrated the Court's commitment to the guidelines it established in the case. In cases like *Goldwater v. Carter*, 444 U.S. 996 (1979) the Court dismissed a case about whether President Carter could end a treaty with Taiwan without consultation with the Senate as a political question.[52] In *Gilligan v. Morgan*, 413 U.S. 1 (1973) the Court dismissed as a political question the complaint about the deaths of antiwar protestors at Kent State University that were attributed to the government's training of the National Guard.[53] The Court also dismissed the following cases that presented the political question of whether the United States can fund or participate in undeclared war: *Crockett v. Reagan*, 720 F. 2d 1355 (D.C. Cir. 1983); *DaCosta v. Larid*, 471 F. 2d 1146 (2d Cir. 1973); *Head v. Nixon*, 342 F Supp. 521 (E.D. La.), affirmed 468 F. 2d 951 (5th Cir. 1972).[54]

One of the most recent cases in which the Court used the political question doctrine is *Walter Nixon v. United States*, 506 U.S. 224 (1993).[55] The Court was asked to determine the constitutionality of Senate procedures to impeach and convict a federal judge. The Court determined a "contro-versy is nonjusticiable—i.e., involves a political question—where there is a textually demonstrable commitment of the issue to a coordinate politi-cal department."[56] In other words when the case involves a political question that another branch of government may have the Constitu-tional authority to resolve, the Court generally does not review the case. Therefore, the Court in *Walter Nixon v. United States* would not hear the case because it said the Constitution gives the Senate "the sole Power to try all impeachment."[57]

2000 Election Crisis and Separation of Powers

The *Bush v. Gore* case met the criteria of the political question doctrine that the Court established in *Baker v. Carr*. Legal analysts assert in *Bush v. Gore* there was a textually demonstrable constitutional commitment of the issue for another political branch to resolve.[58] They argue the Court should have been consistent with its practice of upholding the political question doctrine and defer the 2000 election dispute to another branch.

Some scholars have even argued that the justiciability doctrine of "ripe-ness" should have served as a constraint on the Court from reviewing the case. Ripeness means the issues are still developing or changing and are therefore too premature for judicial review. "The Court did not wait for Florida to complete the process of appointing electors or for Congress to review the validity of Florida's electoral votes. Thus, the critical justiciabil-ity issue in Bush was ripeness."[59] Justice Souter in his dissent in *Bush v. Gore*, discussed the lack of "ripeness" and argued if the Court had not ac-cepted the case, "there would ultimately have been no issue requiring our review."[60] Whether the correct analysis of justiciability in this case was ripeness or the political question doctrine, the conclusion is the same in both assessments; another branch should have decided the election dis-pute, not the High Court. Former Justice Bork noted these doctines limit the Court's role in our democratic system of government. He wrote:

> All of the doctrines that cluster about Article III—not only standing
> but mootness, ripeness, political question, and the like—relate in part,
> and in different though overlapping ways, to an idea, which is more
> than an intuition but less than a rigorous and explicit theory, about
> the constitutional and prudential limits to the powers of an unelected,
> unrepresentative judiciary in our kind of government.[61]

The Court, in the 2000 election crisis, ignored the principles of separa-tion of powers and the political question doctrine that limit the judiciary's power in political matters. This brings us to the question of how did the Supreme Court evolve into the authoritative interpreter of the U.S. Constitution? The Court has taken an active role in government. But what role did the framers intend the judiciary to have in the American system of government?

THE JUDICIARY IN THE AMERICAN POLITICAL SYSTEM

There was little debate during the Constitutional Convention on judicial review. The deliberations on the Court focused on the structure, not the work, of the federal judiciary. There was agreement on the establishment of the U.S. Supreme Court, but there was disagreement on whether there should be lower federal courts. Federalists favored lower federal courts, whereas state-rights supporters maintained state courts should have original jurisdiction, then appeals can be made to the U.S. Supreme Court. Their compromise was the enactment of Article III, which established the U.S. Supreme Court and gave Congress the authority to create lower federal courts.[62] The federalists would later obtain more power for the federal court system at the First Congress.[63]

The First Congress enacted the Judiciary Act of 1789 which created federal courts lower than the U.S. Supreme Court.[64] Section 25 of the Act expanded the federal judiciary's jurisdiction and power to review cases from the state courts that are based on the U.S. Constitution, statutes and treaties. Scholars maintain that although the term judicial review is not stated in Article III and the Judiciary Act, the power of the federal judiciary to review lower court decisions is implied in these laws.[65] It is also clear the framers in their discussion about the federal judiciary favored judicial review. For example, Hamilton argued in the Federalist Papers that one branch of the new government should safeguard the Constitution and its democratic principles, and the unelected branch of government should be granted that authority.[66] The power of the federal judiciary to review lower court decisions with a Constitutional question as well as the Court's review of acts of Congress and the president, evolved over a period of time.[67]

Judicial Review

Judicial review was not established until almost thirty years after the Supreme Court was created.[68] The Court's power was first asserted in the case of *Marbury v. Madison*, 1 Cranch 137 (1803). The Court's ruling that an act of Congress was unconstitutional, served to establish the power of the judiciary in the new government.

There are several landmark constitutional challenges of the Supreme Court's power that helped to establish the Court's authority to interpret the U.S. Constitution.[69] These significant cases include: *Marbury v. Madison*, 1 Cranch 137 (1803),[70] *Martin v. Hunter's Lessee*, 1 Wheaton 304 (1816),[71] *Cohens v. Virginia* 6 Wheaton 264 (1821),[72] *Youngstown Sheet and Tube Co. v. Sawyer*, 343 U.S. 579 (1952),[73] *United States v. Nixon*, 418 U.S. 683 (1974),[74] *Bowsher v. Synar*, 478 U.S 714 (1986),[75] *United States v. United States District Court*, 407 U.S. 297 (1972),[76] and *Immigration and Naturalization Service v. Chadha*, 462 U.S 919 (1983).[77]

Judicial review continues to be controversial because it is not expressly described in the Constitution.[78] There has been no shortage of commentary on whether judicial review should be active or restrained in our demcoracy.[79] Advocates of judicial restraint claim in reviewing cases justices should only consider the law to avoid political and personal interests in their decision making. Judicial activists argue that the Court is an unelected branch and can therefore consider factors outside the law to reach decisions.[80] The framers may have provided some guidance on how active or restrained justices should be in Federalist Paper No. 78.[81]

Framers' Intent of the Judiciary and Judicial Independence

The words of Alexander Hamilton in the *Federalist Papers* shed light on early American political thought on judicial restraint. Hamilton wrote that justices "should be bound down by strict rules and precedents . . . in every particular case."[82] Hamilton does not articulate an extreme view of judicial restraint or judicial activism by our justices. He wrote, "They ought to regulate their decisions by the fundamental laws, rather than by those which are not fundamental."[83] Scholars maintain Hamilton's discussion of judicial review is more closely aligned with principles of judicial restraint.

The framers acknowledged that judicial restraint, where justices base their decision solely on the law, does not always occur. Hamilton addressed these concerns during the ratification of the Constitution when anti-Federalists argued justices could interpret the law based on personal interests instead of the legislature's intent. Hamilton pointed out the Court "must declare the sense of the law; and if they should be disposed to exercise 'will' instead of 'judgment,' the consequence would equally be the substitution of their pleasure to that of the legislative body."[84] If, as Hamilton admits, the

Court could interpret a case based on "will" instead of "judgment," the critical question becomes, how do we distinguish between the two in the judicial decision of a case—specifically a presidential election dispute? In particular, was the *Bush v. Gore* decision, which decided the outcome of the presidential election in 2000, one such occasion where judicial independence was affected?

Judicial independence was debated by the framers extensively in their discussion about the Court. The conflict in the ratification debates on the judiciary was primarily centered on whether the federal court or the state court could be trusted to be independent in its decisions.[85] The framers believed that the Court must be independent to declare acts unconstitutional.[86]

The framers may have hoped for complete judicial independence, but our legal system is only partially autonomous. If judicial autonomy is defined as impartiality, independent of political and social influences, decisions grounded in law, the requirements have not all been met. Complete judicial independence in decision making is an ideal, not the reality. Hamilton, in describing the importance of judicial independence qualified it with the word "complete."[87] In other words, partial independence was not their desire, but a complete independence in interpreting the laws.

The framers were fearful of the judiciary being influenced by extralegal factors that they spent a considerable amount of time debating how to safeguard the "independent spirit in the judges."[88] The framers included significant provisions in their design of the Court to ensure independence. Judges were granted lifetime appointment in an effort to ensure decision making by the Court would never be influenced by political pressures, personal interests, or public repercussion once they left the bench.[89] The framers also created a fix-salaried provision for the judiciary that the legislature can increase for inflation but can never decrease their salary. Their goal was to prevent the legislative branch from having any influence over the judicial branch through financial appropriation.[90] However, these judicial safeguards did not guarantee a truly independent judiciary in the 2000 presidential election dispute. The Court's review of *Bush v. Gore* departed from historical practices of separation of powers and federalism, which suggests extralegal factors, may have affected the judicial independence of the Court.[91]

2000 Election Crisis and Judicial Authority

The five majority justices[92] in *Bush v. Gore* have been accused by voters and the legal community of partisanship because most of the majority justices' record on equal protection was different from their interpretation of the clause in the 2000 election dispute.[93] Howard Gillman established some guidelines to determine partisanship:

> What distinguishes a claim of judicial partisanship . . . are those where judges (a) make decisions consistent with their political affiliations that (b) received no support from judges with different party loyalties and that (c) seem inconsistent with the judges' usual pattern of decision making or with generally accepted understanding of the existing law.[94]

Former Supreme Court Clerk Alan Dershowitz noted that in a presidential election where the Supreme Court Justices voted as citizens, their personal and partisan interests may influence judicial independence without reference in the decision to their particular concerns.[95] In other words, even in reference to legal principles in the decision, the Rehnquist majority could have made a political decision and justified it with selective application of legal rules or principles.[96] Hamilton acknowledged that in some cases, "the courts, on the pretense of a repugnancy, may substitute their own pleasure to the constitutional intentions of the legislature."[97] Many legal analysts argue the Supreme Court's interpretation of the law in the 2000 election dispute reflected a substitution of interests over the legislature's intent.

> The Court's role and decision in the 2000 presidential election dispute was inconsistent with the historical practices of the Court and the framers' intent of separation powers and federalism—none of which designated the Court as the authority to resolve presidential election dispute. *Bush v. Gore* usurped the very essence of these fundamental constitutional principles. The Court was not designed by the framers to have a role in the outcome of a presidential election. Even "James Madison, in recording his own views of the constitutional debate as to how the president should be elected, dismissed selection by the appointed judiciary as 'out of the question.' "[98]

The four dissenting justices in *Bush v. Gore* best shed light on who should resolve a presidential election dispute in the following statement:

> The majority today departs from three venerable rules of judicial restraint that have guided the Court throughout its history. On questions of state law, we have consistently respected the opinions of the highest courts of the states. On questions whose resolution is

committed at least in large measure to another branch of the Federal Government, we have construed our own jurisdiction narrowly and exercised it cautiously. On federal constitutional questions that were not fairly presented to the court whose judgment is being reviewed, we have prudently declined to express an opinion.[99]

WHO HAS THE FINAL AUTHORITY TO RESOLVE PRESIDENTIAL ELECTION DISPUTES?

There is guidance historically and constitutionally on who has the authority to resolve presidential election disputes. In both instances, Congress is the final authority to determine a state's presidential electoral votes.[100] Congress is designated as the branch of government that resolves presidential election disputes based on Constitutional provisions of the Twelfth Amendment and Article II and the political question doctrine that the Court historically used to limit its review of political questions.[101] Even Justice Breyer in his dissent of the *Bush v. Gore* decision argued the Electoral Count Act gives Congress, not the Supreme Court, the authority to resolve electoral disputes.[102]

Historically, the Court has limited its role in resolving political matters. The Florida State Legislature acknowledged the Court's tradition in its *amicus* brief which cited *Baker v. Carr* to demonstrate the political questions presented in *Bush v. Gore* were designated for another branch of government to resolve, not the Court.[103] The legislature maintained, "The High Court's involvement in a political issue that involves the people's will is to be determined, according to law, by another branch that directly represents the people's will."[104]

The democratic principle of separation of powers should limit the Court's role in political disputes. Many scholars believe the Court usurped the authority of the legislative branch to resolve the presidential election dispute. Even Justice Breyer in his dissent of the 2000 election Supreme Court decision wrote, "Congress as the representative body can best express the people's will, and the people's will is what elections are about."[105] Former Supreme Court Clerk Alan Dershowitz made observations that the court has no role in how the president should be elected:

The Constitution, after all, places the power to elect our president in every institution of government but the judiciary. The people vote for electors. The electors vote for the president. If this process produces no clear winner, then the Constitution (and the laws enacted pursuant to it) assigns varying roles to the Senate, the House of Representatives, the state legislatures, and even the governors.[106]

Therefore, the Supreme Court should not have a similar role in any future presidential election dispute. The legislative branch of government is the final arbiter to resolve presidential electoral disputes.

Chapter 7

Reforming America's Broken Electoral System

Man's capacity for justice makes democracy possible, but his inclination to injustice makes democracy necessary.

Reinhold Niebuhr

There is an urgent need to reform America's broken electoral system. Our democracy is at risk. The electoral system is collapsing under the weight of the complexities of election procedures and unregulated election processes.[1] Every election in this decade has been marred by voting problems that dilute the vote. A free election is the heart of a democracy. Yet citizens in more than half the states continue to face huge obstacles to register, cast a vote, and have their votes counted. America must reform its elections procedure and process to expand the electorate and strengthen its democracy.

UNSUCCESSFUL ELECTION REFORM EFFORTS

Since the 2000 presidential debacle, there have been a few attempts to reform the ailing electoral system. Congress enacted the Help America Vote Act (HAVA) of 2002 to help states overhaul their voting technology, and created a new federal agency to oversee the process. The problem with the Act is that HAVA only provides voluntary standards for elections. It does not even require states to use the federal-certified voting technologies. In addition, HAVA is implemented differently in many states, and votes are being rejected or accepted according to the state's interpretation. State officials seem confused on how to interpret and follow its guidelines. Some officials have improperly demanded identification from every voter, when HAVA only mandated it for voters using provisional ballots. One critic has noted, "In the absence of compulsory and explicit national rules, this well-intended law might become in some places, the "Help Some Americans Not to Vote Act."[2]

There have been other unsuccessful attempts in Congress to address election reform. The Senate Committee on Rules and Administration conducted a hearing in 2001 to reform elections. It took testimonies from voting and civil rights organizations, election administrators, and scholars. The hearing focused on voting systems, voter registration, accessibility, voter education, and training of poll workers and election administration. Another Congressional hearing was the Senate Committee on Commerce, Science and Transportation. It also held a hearing in 2001 to hear testimonies from state secretaries, members of Congress, and organizations that represent minorities. No solution emerged from these hearings to reform elections.

The lack of federal action to reform the electoral system has led to a growing grassroots voter protection movement. Various election activists and groups are pushing for reform, such as People for the American Way, The Brennan Center for Justice, VerifiedVoting.org, BlackBoxVoting.org, Moveon.org, and VotersUnite. Most notable is the effort of a "coalition of fifty political, environmental, and social justice groups calling themselves the Pro-Democracy Campaign [and] hammered out a Voters' Bill of Rights petition, which has been signed by eighty-nine organizations."[3]

None of these reform efforts fully addresses the broad range of problems in the broken electoral system. Elections are still increasingly plagued with unreliable and insecure voting machines, voter registration problems, and untrained poll workers that have all prevented citizens' votes from being counted.

EFFECTIVE ELECTION REFORM SOLUTIONS

Election reform attempts have failed for a number of reasons. They lack a comprehensive approach to all the problems in the electoral system. America's electoral system is broken—in every facet of the process. Any effective reform effort must address the following barriers to having our votes counted.[4]

Implement National Uniform Voting Standards

There should be uniform voting standards nationwide for presidential elections. There is no federal standard for citizens in each state voting in the same national election. Instead there are different procedures in different states and counties for the same national election. This lack of uniform standard significantly determines whether your vote will count in a national election.

> In a single state there may be dozens of unique voting systems in use. And even where machines are similar, laws can vary dramatically from district to district, meaning a ballot produced in one district can look entirely different from that of the neighboring county or borough. In some cases, voting equipment and procedure [are] not even uniform across one county.[5]

Uniform national standards would provide equal protection to all voters. It will eliminate the disparities in election procedures in the same precinct, county, and state. To ensure equality, any election reform effort to establish a uniform national standard must be inclusive of all areas in the election process, from voting technology and identification requirements, to absentee and provisional ballots, and voter registration procedures.[6] It will provide fairness to the process that has increasingly become partisan. More importantly, uniform national standards will also help to restore voter confidence in the process.

Register Voters on Election Day

The second most significant barrier to voting is the registration process. Registration rules and procedures are preventing eligible citizens from voting.[7] Voters are being incorrectly purged from voter rolls, and missing or inaccurate voter information in statewide databases prevent voters on Election Day from participating in the democratic process. Elections in a democratic society should encourage voter participation in the political process, but current registration requirements literally turn legitimate voters away at the polls. We must stop these burdensome requirements.

One solution to the nationwide voter registration chaos would be to allow Election Day Registration (EDR). About eight states already have EDR. These states have a higher-than-average voter turnout. In addition, there is no evidence of voter fraud in these states.

> States with EDR have 5–7 percent higher voter turnout. That's an astounding jump, far higher than even the best voter registration or GOTV drive could muster. Recently Iowa and Montana joined six other states with EDR, and North Carolina is poised to be the ninth. Drives are underway in a half dozen other states.[8]

EDR would reduce the growing registration barriers that make it difficult and problematic for eligible citizens to vote.

Enforcement of the Voting Rights Act

Voter intimidation and discrimination have become common in our elections, in part, because the Voting Rights Act is not strictly enforced and Section 5 limits its protection.[9] Section 5 is considered limited in protection because it applies only to "covered jurisdictions" (places with a history of discriminatory practices) not the entire country. The Voting Rights Act must have widespread enforcement to effectively prevent disenfranchisement. Studies show that numerous localities beyond the "covered jurisdiction" in Section 5 have discriminatory practices that violate the law. Therefore, the government needs to better enforce the Act as election procedures in some jurisdictions violate the rights of eligible citizens. The right to vote is fundamental in a democratic system of government.

Appoint Nonpartisan State Election Administrators

At the center of the two most recent presidential election debacles is the partisanship of Republican secretaries of state in Florida and Ohio. Both state secretaries, who were responsible for election administration for their states, also worked as co-chairs of the Republican presidential campaign. Accusations of partisanship and partiality surfaced in the 2000 presidential election when Florida's Secretary of State Kathleen Harris would not allow counties to conduct a recount of the votes as requested by Democrats; and in the 2004 presidential election when Ohio's Secretary of State Kenneth Blackwell would not count provisional ballots for technical reasons, mostly cast by Democrats. The motives and actions of these election executives continue to haunt the election integrity of their respective states. One author wrote, "The Secretary of [State] . . . must be a Secretary for all of us, regardless of party affiliation."[10] To rebuild the voter's trust in the integrity of our elections, election administrators should not work for political parties or serve on presidential campaigns. It is important that their activities are nonpartisan in nature.

Improve Voting Technology

Voting technology must be easier and more reliable for casting and counting the ballots. Technology should improve, not limit voter participation with malfunctioning and insecure machines. In addition, there must be open and transparent elections with paper trails, and random audits. The process should encourage not discourage citizens from participating in the voting process.

Eliminate Privatization in the Election Process

To restore integrity to the election process, Congress must eliminate the privatization of voting machines and the purging of voter registration list.

It was private companies that purged legitimate voters from the voter rolls in Florida's chaotic 2000 presidential election. It was private companies that manufactured and programmed the problematic voting machines in Ohio's 2004 presidential election and other recent elections. The government, not private companies, should administer the purging of voter lists and have strict control of the manufacture and programming of our voting machines.

Our democracy is at a critical crossroads. The integrity of elections in America is waning. Our political leaders must fix this fundamental aspect of our democratic system of government. As another presidential election approaches leaders must act with deliberate swiftness to protect the vote. Our electoral system will only be restored with decisive actions by our national leaders that seek to ensure that all votes are counted.

Chapter 8

Your Rights: What Every Voter Should Know

We are under a Constitution, but the Constitution is what the judges say it is.

Chief Justice Charles Evans Hughes

The heart of the American democratic system of government lies in the electoral process.[1] The most basic constitutional right of its citizens is to participate in the democratic process of voting. Moreover, the rights to have those votes counted are fundamental aspects of our democracy. The Supreme Court upheld this principle in *Reynolds v. Sims* when it said, "The right to vote freely for the candidate of one's choice is the essence of a democratic society and any restriction on that right strike at the heart of representative government."[2] However, America has had a long history of struggles with voting rights.

Universal franchise has been an area of controversy and strife since the founding days of the nation. Many states, in early America, had their own voting requirements that disenfranchised women, blacks, and poor white males. When the U.S. Constitution was enacted the framers did not include any voting rights provisions. After tumultuous years of voting rights conflict, America enacted Amendments to the Constitution to protect its citizens.[3] The Equal Protection and Due Process Clauses of the Fourteenth Amendment protect the right to vote. In addition, various federal statutes, case laws (court decisions), and state laws protect the voter.

This chapter empowers voters about their rights while casting a ballot and enlightens them on whether their ballot is protected after it is cast. The chapter identifies and explains the laws that are aimed at protecting the voter, such as the Equal Protection and Due Process Clauses of the

Fourteenth Amendment, the Voting Rights Act, Voter's Bill of Rights and State laws, the Help America Vote Act (HAVA), the National Voter Registration Act, the Civil Rights Act, and case laws.

THE FOURTEENTH AMENDMENT
AND CASE LAW

In seminal cases that sought to deny or restrict the right to vote, the Supreme Court established the rights of each citizen in case law. In *Harper v. Virginia Bd. of Elections*, the Court established a pivotal right that is denied in the use of punch-card and electronic machines that malfunction and reject votes: "[O]nce the franchise is granted to the electorate, lines may not be drawn which are inconsistent with the Equal Protection Clause of the Fourteenth Amendment."[4] It must be remembered that the Court also declared "the right of suffrage can be denied by a debasement or dilution of the weight of a citizen's vote just as effectively as by wholly prohibiting the free exercise of the franchise."[5] In a national election, votes in a particular jurisdiction can easily be diluted by the use of voting machines that failed to work, flip votes, or cannot produce a verifiable printable ballot for a recount.

The rules and circumstances that govern voting are as important as the act of voting. In *United States v. Mosley* the Court said, "It is as equally unquestionable that the right to have one's vote counted is as open to protection . . . as the right to put a ballot in a box."[6] Various case laws speak to the protection of the ballot after it is cast. The Court asserted in *United States v. Classic* that "Obviously included within the right to choose, secured by the Constitution, is the right of qualified voters within a state to cast their ballots and have them counted."[7] In *Reynolds v. Sims*, the Court acknowledged that citizens have a constitutionally protected right to cast their ballots ". . . and to have their votes counted."[8] The use of electronic machines without verifiable paper trail for a recount denies voters the right to ensure their votes are correctly counted.

There may be a strong basis for an election challenge if a state uses voting machines with high rejection rates in some counties, but in other counties uses better technology with far lower error rates. Studies from the 2000 and 2004 presidential elections reveal that citizens who used inferior voting machines were disenfranchised while other voters that used state-of-the-art technology were more likely to have their votes counted. A federal district court ruled that with punch-card voting systems "people in different counties have significantly different probabilities of having their votes counted; solely because the nature of the system used in their jurisdiction . . . does not afford the 'equal dignity owed to each voter.' "[9] In electronic voting machines, like the punch-card machines, two eligible citizens that reside in different places in the state have different chances of having their votes counted. The disparity in the reliability and accuracy of electronic voting machines violate the right to vote and denies equal protection to voters whose ballots are not counted. Moreover, voters are treated differently with the use of five different voting machines used in the electoral system.

The disparate treatment of provisional and absentee ballots in recent elections according to where one lives also violates our Constitution. The High Court said in *Harper* v. *Virginia Bd. of Elections*, "The right to vote is protected in more than the initial allocation of the franchise. Equal protection applies as well to the manner of its exercise. Having once granted the right to vote on equal terms, the State may not, by later arbitrary and disparate treatment, value one person's vote over that of another."[10] The 2004 presidential election survey sponsored by the federal Election Assistance Commission and performed by the Election Data Services found a disparate treatment of a disproportionate number of 2004 provisional ballots nationwide were not all counted according to different rules in various states.

EQUAL PROTECTION CLAUSE

The Equal Protection Clause has been used in several recent election disputes. After the 2000 presidential election, numerous lawsuits used the clause to challenge voting systems.[11] Most of these cases have been successful and led to the prohibition of the punch-card voting systems that diminished voters' chances of having their votes counted. Similar efforts to use the Equal Protection Clause to challenge current problematic voting systems could either lead to reforms or prohibit their use in a democratic election.

The most controversial equal protection case in the nation's history was perhaps the *Bush v. Gore* case. The Rehnquist majority's equal protection application in *Bush v. Gore* was unprecedented. An assessment of this seminal case is paramount in any discussion of the Equal Protection Clause.

Bush v. Gore: Equal Protection Violations

The majority found three equal protection violations with the Florida Supreme Court's order.[12] First, the U.S. Supreme Court found the statewide recount efforts violated the Equal Protection Clause because the Florida court did not establish a uniform standard to determine legal votes. The Court pointed out that the constitutional problem raised by Bush is that one county with a liberal set of rules might count an undervote as legal and another county under a conservative set of rules might discard a similar ballot. Second, the majority was also concerned that the Florida court

did not grant recount observers the right to object to discrepancies or identify who would count the ballots.[13] Third, the High Court found a violation
of the Equal Protection Clause in the effort to recount only undervotes:

> As a result the citizen whose ballot was not read by a machine because
> he failed to vote for a candidate in a way readable by a machine may
> still have his vote counted in a manual recount; on the other hand,
> the citizen who marks two candidates in a way discernable by the
> machine will not have the same opportunity to have his vote count,
> even if a manual examination of the ballot would reveal the requisite
> indicia of intent.[14]

The dissenting justices argued against the equal protection claims to
which the decision was based. Justice Breyer challenged the three equal
protection claims of the majority:

> In a system that allows counties to use different types of voting sys-
> tems, voters already arrive at the polls with an unequal chance that
> their votes will be counted. I do not see how the fact that this results
> from counties' selection of different voting machines, rather than a
> court order, makes the outcome any more fair. Nor do I understand
> why the Florida Supreme Court's recount order, which helps to re-
> dress this inequity, must be entirely prohibited based on a deficiency
> that could easily be remedied.[15]

The impact of the *Bush v. Gore* decision on the American system of government is evident in various cases that used the equal protection precedent from the case to challenge voting systems. It is clear the equal
protection jurisprudence from *Bush v. Gore* has influenced election law
cases, although the Court limited its decision. As more citizens challenge
voting systems using the *Bush v. Gore* precedent, equal protection protections may evolve in our democracy.

DUE PROCESS CLAUSE

The Due Process Clause of the Fourteenth Amendment also protects
the voter. The clause gives voters a right to have their ballots counted in an
election process that is fundamentally fair.[16] The Due Process Clause includes a "substantive" as well as a "procedural" component. Procedural
due process involves a standard of fairness. It denies government the
power to deny voting rights through election procedures. Therefore, counties cannot conduct an election and develop vote counting procedures that

deny voters their rights. Procedural due process was initially the only due process in our jurisprudence. The Due Process Clause eventually evolved into a "substantive" component. Substantive due process "bar[s] certain government actions regardless of the fairness of the procedures used to implement them."[17] There are several case laws that speak to fairness in the election process such as *Duncan v. Poythress, Griffin v. Burns, Marks v. Stinson, McKye v. State Election Bd. of State of Oklahoma, Bonas v. Town of N. Smithfield, Siegel v. Lepore*.[18] These court decisions all found that there is a violation of substantive due processes when there is fundamental unfairness in the election process.

In the 2000 and 2004 presidential election disputes, the principle of due process involved the question of fairness to voters that attempted to cast ballots in the election. There were concerns about procedural due process when punch-card voting machines in some counties failed to count votes because of its high rejection rate of ballots. In the 2000 election crisis, candidate Al Gore raised the issue of procedural fairness in his case, as well as the Florida Supreme Court in its decision that called for a statewide recount.[19] Bush also asked the Supreme Court in the 2000 presidential election if the method of counting votes in the Florida election violated the Due process and Equal Protection Clauses of the Fourteenth Amendment. The High Court ruled on the equal protection claim of Bush and not on the Due process challenge. Some legal analysts observed the substantive aspect of due process in the 2000 election with the punch-card voting systems crisis involved the fundamental right to vote. One analyst noted, "Only by ignoring the substantive content of the right to vote and focusing instead solely on the comparative treatment of ballots could the Court reach its desired outcome."[20]

Since the 2000 election crisis, the court has made it clear that the Due Process Clause also extends to fair recounting procedures.[21] In a recent election dispute the court stated in *Miller v. County Comm'n* that "inherent in the recount procedure is the concept of fairness to all interested candidates in an election . . . a recount plays an integral and indispensable role tantamount to fundamental principles of due process, which cannot be ignored or omitted."[22] Therefore, voting on electronic machines with no verifiable paper trail undermines fundamental principles of fairness and due process. A recount with some form of a paper trail is a fair method to discover problems in the election process.

FEDERAL STATUTES

There are various Federal statutes that seek to protect citizens' right to vote. These election safeguards were established within the last 40 years to protect voters in state and federal elections. Special provisions have also been adapted to some of these statutes in recent years to further ensure the rights of voters.

Voting Rights Act

The Voting Rights Act of 1965, to which provisions have been added over the years, was enacted to prevent states from denying voters their rights based on their ethnicity, race or language. The Act prohibits any person from "failing or refusing to permit any qualified person from voting in . . . Federal elections; refusing to count the vote of a qualified person; or intimidating anyone attempting to vote or anyone who is assisting a person in voting."[23] The Voting Rights Act does not require evidence of intentional discrimination, and it does not require proof of conspiracy to demonstrate violation of the Act. In *Mobile v. Bolden* when the Court ruled purposeful discrimination was required to show a violation, Congress revised Section 2 to insist it is the results of the election procedures and process that determine violations, not the intent.[24] Therefore, it is the problems in the electoral system in recent presidential elections that determine violations, not whether the state intentionally discriminated against minorities. The various studies on spoiled ballots and the personal testimonies of minorities present convincing evidence of violations of the Act.

Voting rights expert Allan Lichtman[25] testified at a U.S. Commission on Civil Rights Tallahassee hearing that a violation of the Voting Rights Act occurs if there are the following disparities:

> Differences in voting procedures and voting technologies between white areas and minority areas and if voting procedures and voting technologies used in minority areas give minorities less opportunities to have their votes counted . . . If your vote isn't being tallied, that in effect is like having your franchise denied fundamentally.[26]

A citizen's right to participate in the democratic process of voting can be denied just as easily by procedural barriers to voting, as well as voting machines with high rejection rates, or that are unreliable and insecure.[27] A state's election process violate Section 2 of the Voting Rights Act if their procedures dilute the opportunities for minorities to vote for the candidate of their choice.[28] If citizens are denied certain rights in the democratic process of voting, as a result of unreliable and insecure electronic machines, voters could perhaps use the Voting Rights Act in their claims in court.

Help America Vote Act

Congress enacted the Help America Vote Act (HAVA) with various provisions that protect voters in state and federal elections. HAVA aims to change the practice of disparate voting systems in the states by requiring improvement in voting machines, election procedures, registration processes, and poll worker training. The objective of the Act is described in its opening paragraph:

> To establish a program to provide funds to states to replace punch-card voting systems, to establish the Election Assistance Commission to assist in the administration of Federal elections and to otherwise provide assistance with the administration of certain Federal election laws and programs, to establish minimum election administration standards for States and units of local government with responsibility for the administration of Federal elections, and for other purposes.[29]

HAVA protects voters by establishing requirements for voting and voter registration in the states. After the widespread problems about voter registration that occurred in recent elections, the Act stipulated that by 2006 voters must be given a provisional ballot if their names are not listed on voter rolls. It also protects voters by requiring states to maintain a statewide database of voter registration information. The confirmation of voter registration was one of the most problematic areas of voting in the 2000 election fiasco. Additionally, HAVA established a new federal agency to assist with election administration. National elections were without any federal regulation of the process, which proved problematic in recent elections.

HAVA is not without its problems in the implementation phase, and voters should be aware of the problems with the Act. Congress provided federal funding but does not fully fund the Act, which affects the ability of some localities to implement it. Nevertheless, HAVA was signed into law by President Bush in 2002 to establish new federal requirements to protect the right to vote and to have that vote counted.

Other Federal Statutes

There are provisions in other federal statutes that protect the voter. The Civil Rights Act of 1968 is one such statute that can appropriately be used to protect voters with claims of discrimination and intimidation in elections. According to Section 245 of Title 18 of the Civil Rights Act, it is illegal "for any person to willfully . . . injure, intimidate or interfere with any person' or attempt such injury, intimidation or interference 'in order to intimidate such person or any other person or any class of person from voting or qualifying to vote.' "[30]

One study on the 2004 election problems assert that the 1993 National Voter Registration Act (NVRA),[31] often referred to as the motor voter law, also protects voters. Voter registration has become problematic in recent elections with many eligible voters wrongfully turned away at the polls. The Act requires states to have fair procedures to register voters. "Pursuant to NVRA, Section 1974a of Title 42 makes it a crime for any person to willfully steal, destroy, conceal, mutilate, or alter any voting records including those having to do with voter registration."[32] These statutes make it clear that procedures that obstruct citizens from registering, or deprive voters from participating in the election process are criminal offenses.[33]

STATE LAWS

States have election laws with specific provision and procedures to ensure a fair election. Many states also have statutory recount provisions to protect the fairness and integrity of elections. Voters should become familiar with the elections codes in their state. Additionally, many states have a voter's bill of rights that outlines specific protection for voters. Citizens in recent presidential elections encountered voting problems that denied them of rights that were clearly outlined in their state's bill of rights. Voters should contact their local elections office to obtain a copy to empower themselves on Election Day.

These voters' bill of rights are very specific and address a wide range of voting problems that often occur at the polls. Protections from these problems are guaranteed by the state in which the voter resides. The following excerpts from various states' bill of rights illustrate what every voter should know.

You have the right to vote without any person trying to influence your vote and to vote in a booth that prevents others from watching you mark your ballot. You have the right to remain in the voting booth for five minutes if there are other voters waiting and for 10 minutes if there are no other voters waiting. You have the right to receive up to two replacement ballots if you make a mistake and spoil your ballot. If at any time before you finally cast your ballot, you feel you have made a mistake, you have the right to exchange the spoiled ballot for a new ballot. You have the right to ask questions of the precinct board and election officials regarding election procedures and to receive an answer or be directed to the appropriate official for an answer. You have the right to cast a provisional ballot if your name is not listed on the voting rolls. You have the right to cast a ballot if you are present and in line at the polling place prior to the close of the polls. You have the right to cast a secret ballot free from intimidation. You have the right to receive a new ballot if, prior to casting your ballot, you believe you made a mistake.[34]

Knowledge of these voters' bill of rights by an informed citizen better ensures that your franchise will not be denied and your vote will count. The right to vote in a free election is the most fundamental aspect of a democratic society. It is vital that citizens in a democracy are aware of the legal principles that protect those rights. The Equal Protection Clause of the Fourteenth Amendment, the Voting Rights Act, Voters Bill of Rights, and HAVA all aim to protect the voter. This knowledge has become particularly important in light of recent election problems where voters were denied their right to vote and were unaware of their rights. An awareness of these laws can empower voters and better ensure election integrity in our democracy.

Appendix A

Election Protection Coalition: *2008 Presidential Primary Report: Looking Ahead to November*

VOTERS' COMPLAINTS: EXCERPTS

The full report is available at: http://nationalcampaignforfairelections .org/. Reprinted with permission.

California

A poll worker in Baldwin Park was going down a long line of voters demanding they show identification before they could vote, despite no identification being required.

- Callers reported that they did not receive the vote-by-mail ballots they had previously requested.
- At one polling place, a poll worker challenged a student voter's right to vote and refused to issue a regular ballot because the poll worker asserted that the voter no longer lived at the address the voter used for voter registration.
- In Oxnard, a polling place did not have the voter registration roll for any voter with a last name beginning with "M" or later in the alphabet. All voters with a last name beginning with "M" or later

were being instructed to vote by provisional ballot. Poll workers were forcing these voters to vote provisionally.

- Several polling places opened late, making it difficult for working voters to vote prior to going to work and creating confusion for voters.

Georgia

A voter in Cobb County reported the entrance to her precinct was blocked and the polling location appeared to be closed. She explained that police wanted voters to enter through the side of the building, but people were unaware and were leaving.

- There were scattered reports of voters being issued a ballot for the wrong party—one caller reported his girlfriend was given an incorrect ballot and the poll worker refused to provide the correct one.
- Another caller reported she was unable to cast a regular ballot at her polling location because a poll worker had incorrectly marked her name when a previous voter with a similar name had voted. Instead, she was forced to cast a provisional ballot.
- Many voters showed up to vote, believed they were registered, and in some cases had received confirmation of their registration but were told they were not on the rolls.
- Several voters from one particular polling location called to report very long lines caused by the electronic ID verification machines—only two of the ten machines were being used.
- After presenting identification, a caller was told she was listed as having already voted. The poll worker was unable to make the screen function properly and advised her to return later, even though she had already waited an hour. When the caller returned in the evening, she was told she could have voted earlier by paper ballot.

Illinois

Polling places in multiple counties opened late. One voter reported that he could not wait for his polling place to open and would not be able to vote because he worked over one hour away.

- One voter knew that, by law, officials were required to offer Democratic, Republican, and Green Party ballots but did not receive his requested Green Party ballot at his polling location in Lake County until he insisted to multiple officials that they provide him with the correct ballot. After two different officials claimed not to have any ballots, they were "finally able to dig one up."

- A caller expressed concern about the ballot machine at her polling location. When she finished voting, the election judge tried to feed her ballot into the machine back-side up. She protested and the ballot went through the correct way, but the election judge said that she "was one of the lucky ones." The caller was concerned that if the election judge was doing this with other ballots; these ballots were not being counted because they were not being fed into the machine properly.
- When a voter asked for a Democratic ballot in a predominantly Republican area, she was told she needed to show photo identification, contrary to Illinois law. She refused and insisted they allow her to vote. Other poll workers then made loud remarks like, "Oh, we've got a Democrat here."

New York

Multiple callers reported inappropriate behavior by poll workers. One caller reported that her husband, a registered Republican, was laughed at and ridiculed because of his declared party affiliation. Another caller reported a poll worker made a disparaging remark about the candidate for whom she was wearing a pin.

- At a Manhattan theater, a caller reported the only voting machine assigned to his district had broken down. Voters were instructed to fill out emergency ballots at a table without any privacy. Ballots were then folded into quarters and placed in a cardboard box.
- Another caller reported there was a lack of privacy for voters filling out affidavit ballots at her polling place. She was also concerned there was no visible lockbox to hold the completed ballots. Instead, poll workers took the envelope and "disappeared into a room with it."
- A caller reported that at her polling location, poll workers physically entered the voting booth trying to fix the machines and changed the voter's selection. Election Protection sent a Mobile Legal Volunteer to the polling location to inform the poll workers that they needed to use emergency ballots.

District of Columbia

Poll workers at one precinct were giving out Republican and Statehood Green Party ballots to registered Democrats because they had run out of Democratic ballots.

- A caller reported that, when the polling place at Mount Pleasant Library ran out of paper ballots, voters had to wait in a long line because there was only one touch-screen machine. The polling site also ran out of registration cards to submit for a ballot after signing the roster, so people started using blank pieces of paper to obtain ballots.

- One of Election Protection's Mobile Legal Volunteers reported that when she voted the optical scanner at her polling place was not working. Ballots were being placed inside the scanner to be processed later.
- Another caller had voted Democrat and registered as a Democrat since 1986 but was informed at her polling place that she was listed as a Republican and so had to vote on a provisional ballot.

Maryland

A caller in Upper Marlboro reported the ballot on her touch-screen machine was incorrectly set up as an audio ballot. The voter asked the presiding election judge for assistance and, after speaking to his supervisor, pulled the card out of the machine. The screen read that the ballot had been cancelled, and the election judge gave her a provisional ballot and took her voter card. The caller said she witnessed the same incident happen to approximately fifteen to twenty other voters.

- Multiple callers reported long lines due to disorganization at the polling site, an inadequate number of voting machines, or insufficient preparation for check-in. Several callers reported long lines caused a large number of voters to leave without casting a ballot.
- A number of callers reported they had not been notified of polling location changes. A voter in Prince George's County reported she and other voters had stood in line for 30 to 45 minutes before finding out the polling site had changed. Another caller reported she did not know the polling place where she has voted for a number of years had changed until she was waiting in line. She ultimately cast a provisional ballot along with at least four other people in line.

Virginia

A polling place in Fairfax County had only one person checking voters in and one person handing out ballots. At one point, a poll worker even went outside and advised voters that they might want to come back later.

- An Arlington County polling place lacked sufficient parking forcing voters to circle the location for over 30 minutes. The caller observed several voters give up and drive off without casting a ballot.

- Multiple callers reported that a polling place in Prince William County was understaffed and underresourced. Several voters could not wait in a line that took over an hour and left without casting a ballot.
- A polling place in Fairfax County was listed incorrectly on the Website and in the voters' guide mailed by the board of elections, causing numerous voters to go to the wrong location with no information directing them to the correct address.

Ohio

In Cuyahoga County, disability access and electronic reading machines were down at multiple polling locations—some had not worked since early morning. One report noted that the person with knowledge to operate the special disability equipment simply failed to show up.

- The paper ballot system also raised privacy issues across the state. Mobile Legal Volunteers observed multiple polling locations that lacked sufficient privacy screens, forcing many voters to cast their ballot in the open.
- Numerous eligible voters were unable to vote with regular ballots because their names did not appear on the electoral rolls or appeared incorrectly. A caller reported that when she gave the poll worker an electric bill as proof of identification, the worker refused to accept it and told her voters needed a valid Ohio drivers' license with a current address in order to vote.
- One student reported that a poll worker required students to recite their address, while another overheard poll workers incorrectly saying that if the address on a student's driver's license did not match the address on their voter registration they would have to vote a provisional ballot.

Texas

Election Protection received multiple reports of employers denying employees their legal right to time off to vote. One caller reported that, when he requested time to leave and vote, the employer responded, "it's your problem if you do not get off in time to go vote."

- At a polling location in Dallas, a volunteer for a sheriff candidate entered a polling place and started incorrectly telling people waiting in line that if they were voting Republican they could go down the street and vote at a different location.

- A single location had only eight booths and one scanner, but the polling place housed three precincts.
- A polling place in Denton County was directing disabled voters to the back of the building where there was no assistance for them to go up the stairs to the voting area.
- General logistics were a significant problem in Texas. Multiple callers reported tow trucks towing cars, including one site in Dallas where people had to leave the caucus location to go outside to stop their cars from being towed.

Pennsylvania

A number of callers were confused and upset by sample ballots that seemed official but only showed one presidential candidate.

- A voter entered her polling place and asked to be shown how to push the button for her candidate. The poll worker told the voter she was supporting a competitor and said she hoped the voter would adhere to her request.
- Election Protection received a call from a voter who reported that the voting machines at her location were set for Republicans only. She told the poll worker that she was a Democrat and the worker replied, "Not today." The voter insisted that she had always voted at that location as a Democrat, but the poll worker simply said "Oh well." The caller was unable to vote.
- At one location, a sample ballot provided by the city was displayed next to the polling machine. A volunteer for a particular candidate had marked this sample ballot in favor of his candidate. This defaced sample ballot remained on display into the afternoon.
- Election Protection received multiple reports of privacy issues—in one location, polling booths were exposed with the machine screens in plain sight of poll workers.
- Disability access was also an issue in Pennsylvania. One woman reported that her mother was unable to access the polling place which was downstairs—the poll workers refused to provide her with a provisional ballot. Another caller reported that she was not allowed assistance from her husband despite being blind. The situation was mismanaged, and the caller felt publicly embarrassed.
- One voter called to report that, contrary to Pennsylvania law, a poll worker refused to allow her child to accompany her to the voting machine. When she asked the poll worker why her son was not allowed, the poll worker told her it was because her son "can read."

Appendix B

U.S. Commission on Civil Rights, Voting Irregularities in Florida During the 2000 Presidential Election: First-Hand Accounts of Voter Disenfranchisement

EXCERPTS: TESTIMONIES OF VOTERS

The full report is available at www.usccr.gov/pubs/vote2000/report/main.htm.

Citizens Who Were Not Permitted To Vote

Cathy Jackson, an African American woman, has been a registered voter in Broward County since 1996. Upon registering in Broward County, Ms. Jackson was told that if she ever experienced a problem with her voter registration card, she would be allowed to vote if she could produce a valid driver's license. Ms. Jackson voted in Broward without any incident using her driver's license since 1996. However, when she went to her polling place, Precinct 52Z, on November 7, 2000, she was told that her name was not on the list. The poll workers suggested that she travel back to her old precinct in Miami-Dade County to vote. Ms. Jackson did as she was advised even though she had voted in Broward County since she moved from Miami-Dade County in 1996. After waiting 45 minutes at her old precinct, the poll workers in Miami-Dade told Ms. Jackson that her name was not on the rolls and referred her back to Broward to vote.

When Ms. Jackson returned to the Broward precinct, the poll workers advised her to wait while they checked her registration status. While she waited, Ms. Jackson observed a poll worker from another precinct within the same polling place allow an elderly white voter, whose name did not appear on the rolls, to fill out an affidavit and vote. When Ms. Jackson asked if she could do the same, the poll workers explained that she could fill out an affidavit, but that she could not vote until they had verified her registration. The phone lines to the supervisor of elections office, however, remained busy for several hours. Ms. Jackson became upset and eventually left to go to work. Undeterred by these delays, Ms. Jackson returned to her precinct after work to try to vote again, but the poll workers were never able to verify her registration status and refused to allow her to vote.[1]

Donnise DeSouza, an African American, has been registered to vote since 1982 in Miami-Dade County. When she entered the Richmond Fire Station in Miami-Dade County at 6:50 P.M. and showed her identification to the poll worker, Ms. DeSouza was told that her name was not on the rolls. The poll worker directed her to the "problem line," so that her registration status could be verified with the supervisor of elections office. Ms. DeSouza recalled that the line of about fifteen people did not move, but at 7 P.M. when the poll began to close, a poll worker announced to the group "if our name was not on the roll that she could not let us vote and that there was nothing she could do." The poll workers stopped their attempts to verify the registration status of the voters who had been standing in line. When Ms. DeSouza asked if there was an absentee ballot that would allow her to cast her vote, the poll worker explained that there was nothing he could do.

Ms. DeSouza testified to the Commission that she was "very agitated" and the next day began to register complaints with various sources about her experience. Upon further investigation with the office of the supervisor of elections, she discovered that the poll workers should have continued their efforts to resolve the problems of those voters who were in the precinct prior to the 7 P.M. closing time. Furthermore, Ms. DeSouza learned that her name was actually on the rolls of registered voters, because subsequently a worker at the elections office showed her the sheet that contained her name where she should have been allowed to sign. But Ms. DeSouza explained, "at that point [the election was over so] there was nothing they could do and I was deprived of my right to vote."[2]

Angenora Ramsey, an African American former poll worker with 18 years' experience, had changed her address prior to November 7. Based on her familiarity with election procedures, when Ms. Ramsey went to vote at Precinct 62 in Palm Beach County, she completed a change of address affidavit. But when the poll worker tried to call the office of the supervisor of elections to verify Ms. Ramsey's registration status, she was unable to get through. According to Ms. Ramsey, the phone lines remained busy for three and a half hours—a delay she had never experienced during her time as a poll worker. Ultimately, the poll workers refused to allow her to vote because they could not verify her voter status.[3]

Margarita Green, a 75-year-old Cuban American woman, went to vote at the same precinct in Miami-Dade County where she had always voted since becoming a citizen in 1966. When Mrs. Green showed her registration card to the poll worker, she was told that her name was not on the rolls and that she must speak with another poll worker who would look into the problem. Mrs. Green recalled that it took a long time for the poll worker to reach the supervisor of elections because the phone line was busy. When she finally got through, the worker explained that according to their records Mrs. Green had called in 1998 and "erased" herself from the voter list. Although Mrs. Green insisted that she had not called and showed the poll worker her registration card, the poll worker refused to allow her to vote.[4]

R. Jai Howard, vice president of the Florida Agricultural and Mechanical University Student Government Association, testified on behalf of more than twelve thousand predominantly African American students. She described the massive voter registration efforts that took place at the school in the months preceding the November 2000 election. The association's efforts continued until October 10, 2000 (the last day to register before the election) and included a rally in which Reverend Jesse Jackson and Ion Sancho, the Leon County supervisor of elections, participated. Despite its efforts, the Student Government Association learned in the days following the election that large numbers of students had problems voting, "including one student who had two voter registration cards with two different precincts, some students who received no voter registration cards, switching of precincts without prior notification, misinformation at precincts, and students who had attempted to register numerous times and never received registration [cards] and were never entered into the system." As a result of these combined problems, many students who believed they had been properly registered were not allowed to vote.[5]

Ava Zamites of Tampa waited for one and a half hours but could not get through to the supervisor of elections office. In another instance, when **Lynette Johnson** was told that her name was not on the voter list, poll workers attempted to call the supervisor of elections office. When they could not get through for an hour, she had to return to work. She continued to call on her own with no success.

Poll Workers Confirm Widespread
Voter Disenfranchisement

Marilyn Nelson, a poll worker with 15 years of experience in Miami-Dade County, testified, "By far this was the worst election I have ever experienced. After that election I decided I didn't want to work as a clerk anymore." At North Dade Elementary School, Precinct 232, she observed several voters who had presented their voter registration cards showing they were properly registered, but the poll workers did not allow them to vote because their names did not appear on the rolls. Ms. Nelson also saw voters with their "orange cards," which meant that the voter had registered on time and should be allowed to vote, provided that the poll worker could verify the voter's registration status with the supervisor of elections office. Many of these voters, however, were not permitted to vote because the poll workers could not get through on the phone line to the supervisor's office.[6]

Maria DeSoto, a poll worker in Palm Beach County, testified that she used her personal cellular phone to call the supervisor of elections office all day but was only able to get through two or three times over the course of 12 hours. Ms. DeSoto added that if voters' names did not appear on the rolls, they were not allowed to vote, even if they presented valid identification.[7]

Barbara Phoele, a poll worker in Broward County at Precinct 6C, observed mostly African American and Hispanic voters being turned away because their names did not appear on the rolls. The precinct clerk at her site was unable to get through to the central election office to give affidavits to those voters whose names did not appear. According to Ms. Phoele, the clerk did not communicate with the voters and did nothing to encourage them to vote. In fact, Ms. Phoele noticed later that afternoon that the sign informing voters where they should call if they experienced problems had never been posted. She brought this to the attention of the precinct clerk who explained, "I didn't have time to put it up." Ms. Phoele recalled that in past elections it took only about 10 minutes to reach the elections supervisor, but on November 7, 2000, she turned away approximately forty or fifty people because she could not access the supervisor of elections.[8]

Marvin Rickles, Jr., a deputy at Precinct 74B in Palm Beach County, observed an African American school principal turned away, after waiting for two hours, because her name did not appear on the rolls and poll workers could not reach the supervisor of elections office. She returned to the precinct later that afternoon and was allowed to vote only after she discovered that her name had been misspelled on the rolls.[9]

Millard Suid, a poll worker at the Water Works Department in Boynton Beach, testified he was not able to get through to the office of the supervisor of elections. He recalled helping only one voter over the course of about eight hours. Mr. Suid stated that the precinct deputy estimated that poll workers "[m]ust have turned away maybe 30 or 50 people that could not vote."[10]

Randall Benston worked as an area chair overseeing three precincts in Broward County. Mr. Benston observed poll workers who were unaware that voters not on the rolls were allowed to fill out affidavits and vote. He eventually persuaded the poll workers to allow voters to fill out affidavits in accordance with Florida election law.[11]

POLLING PLACES CLOSED EARLY OR MOVED WITHOUT NOTICE

Denise Ballard of Palm Beach County observed poll workers turn away voters at her precinct at 7 P.M., even though they had been in line prior to 7 P.M. Similarly, Ted Dominick of Broward County complained that he arrived at the poll at 6:55 P.M. and was turned away. **John McGuire** of Pinellas County, for example, complained that his polling place, Precinct 509, moved without prior notice.

Polling Places Closed Early

When **Lavonna Lewis**, an African American first-time voter, went to her polling place to vote, she was told by a white poll worker standing outside that the poll was closed. As she turned to leave, the poll worker allowed a white gentleman to walk in and get in line to vote.[12]

Donnise DeSouza arrived at her assigned precinct at 6:30 P.M. but could not enter until 6:50 P.M., due to the long line of cars parked on the street waiting to gain access to the polling place. Once Ms. DeSouza was finally able to enter the polling place, she waited for another 10 minutes while poll workers verified her registration status. At 7 P.M., however, the poll workers announced to Ms. DeSouza and about fifteen other voters who were waiting to be helped that they could not vote because the poll was closed.[13]

Susan and **Joel Newman** arrived at the Water Works Department in Palm Beach to vote at approximately 6:15 P.M. Upon their arrival, they noticed:

[T]he iron gates at the entrance were closed, preventing entrance . . . Several cars pulled into the entrance lane and tried to attract attention by honking horns and ringing an intercom. We waited 5–10 minutes but no one showed up and the gates remained locked. We drove off thinking we were wrong about the closing time—that the polls must have closed at 6:00. A few blocks away we spotted a police car and pulled up to check. He verified that the polls were open until 7:00. We complained about the situation we had just experienced and he told us to go to the Board of Elections (some 20 minutes away). We drove there and met a policeman as we entered the building. He listened to our complaint and politely told us there was nothing he could do. We would have to register our complaint with the [supervisor] of elections, Theresa LePore. Unfortunately, he told us her office had closed at 5 P.M. and her staff went home [and] we would have to complain the following day. We left, realizing that we would have no opportunity to vote this year.[14]

Millard Suid, a poll worker at the Water Works Department on John Road in Boynton Beach, confirmed the above poll closing. He explained that the gates to the property are on an automatic timer that shuts them every day at 6:15 P.M. When the automatic timer shut the gates at 6:15 P.M. on Election Day, however, Mr. Suid stated, "It was a disaster. The people at the Water Works Department should have known about it or the people, Theresa LePore, who runs that particular district, should have known about that." When asked if he called the supervisor of elections to report that the gates had closed, Mr. Suid testified, "That wouldn't do any good, couldn't get in. I had called 911 and told the police. Now there was a young lady at the Water Works Department who worked there all day and she left at like 5:30 and she said, 'I'll be back at 7:30 to lock up.' Now she should have known this gate's going to lock automatically. . . . That wasn't the first time they used that. So somebody screwed up."[15]

Robert Weisman, the county administrator for Palm Beach County, stated in a response to an interrogatory issued by the Commission after the February 16, 2001, hearing that he did not know about the gate-closing incident until the Commission hearing. He further acknowledged that a subsequent investigation by representatives of the supervisor of elections office determined that the gate indeed had closed. Mr. Weisman did not dispute that the automatic locking of the gate blocked access to the Palm Beach County polling place before the official closing.[16]

Polling Places Moved Without Notice

Felix Boyle, a registered voter in Miami-Dade County, described his polling place as a "medieval labyrinth." There were "sulfuric odors from standing water, orange cones, barriers, deep pits, broken concrete. It was a real problem getting there." Although Mr. Boyle's polling place during the primary was very busy, the new location was "deserted" on November 7, 2000. He surmised that the appearance of the site might have resulted in fewer people voting there on Election Day.[17]

NATIONAL VOTER REGISTRATION ACT: THE
MOTOR VOTER LAW

Curtis Gans, director of the Committee for the Study of the American Electorate, testified, "In this election, thousands of people, not only in Florida, but in other places, who registered at motor voter places, motor vehicle license bureaus, and in social service agencies were not on the rolls when they came to vote."[18]

A poll worker who testified at the Commission's Miami hearing corroborated this observation: "[T]here were people who had registered to vote through motor voter and somehow their registration was not transmitted to the supervisor of elections office. I saw that with married couples in my own precinct. One person would be registered to vote, the other person would not. The person who was not registered to vote couldn't vote unless they physically went to the supervisor of elections office and picked up a piece of paper, which they then brought back to me, because we couldn't reach them on the telephone."[19]

Congresswoman Corrine Brown also noted the failure of proper processing of motor voter registration, stating that "thousands of people went and got their driver's license, but to this date they did not . . . receive their voter card."[20]

Marcia and **George Seamans** of Boynton Beach registered to vote at the DHSMV on two occasions and were told at the polls that their names were not on the voter rolls. Although at the DHSMV to obtain their driver's licenses, they were asked to register to vote. They were directed to fill out a separate registration application and, upon its completion, were told they were registered. When they went to the polling place, however, their names were not on the rolls. When the poll worker called the central office to verify their registration status, they learned that their names were not on the central voter file, and they were not allowed to vote.[21]

In response to the Commission's interrogatory regarding the Seamans' registration, Ms. Lambert (director of the Division of Driver Licenses) stated that the Division of Driver Licenses' records confirmed that Mr. and Mrs. Seamans submitted their voter registration applications at the time of obtaining their driver's licenses. The division's records also indicated that their voter registration applications and the transmittal reports were forwarded to the applicable supervisor of elections office. Ms. Lambert, however, was not able to explain the status of their voter registration. She reiterated that all voter registration applications and transmittal reports are forwarded to the supervisor of elections within five days of receipt. With regard to the Seamans, Ms. Lambert explained that voter registration applications are forwarded to Palm Beach County by U.S. mail and that copies of the applications are not maintained in their field driver license offices due to confidentiality. Based on this response, it is impossible to

determine whether the voter registration applications were actually transmitted to the supervisor of elections office or whether that office misplaced
the applications once they were received. Nevertheless, Mr. and Mrs. Seamans properly registered to vote at their driver license office and were
deprived of their right to vote on Election Day.[22]

Bill Zannie of Palm Beach County registered to vote at the DHSMV
when he went to obtain his Florida driver's license. He requested a confirmation to ensure that he was registered to vote. The DHSMV staff assured
him that he was registered. He did not, however, obtain a confirmation.
When he went to vote on the day of the election, he was told that his
name was not on the voter rolls. He also learned that there was no record
of his registration. Because he registered to vote at a governmental agency,
he assumed he was registered properly and to his disappointment, he was
not registered.[23]

When asked about the voter registration status of Mr. Zannie, Sandra
Lambert responded that according to the division's electronic transaction
file for December 7, 1998, the date Mr. Zannie obtained his driver's license
for the first time in Florida, the record indicated that he was currently registered to vote; therefore, DHSMV staff did not forward any forms to the
supervisor of elections. According to Mr. Zannie, December 7, 1998, was
the first time he had obtained a driver's license in Florida and was the first
time he requested to register to vote in the state of Florida. Because the
Division of Driver Licenses' records indicated that he was already registered, it took no action to register him to vote.

Ms. Lambert explained in an answer to the Commission's interrogatory
that in the two times that Mr. Zannie moved in Florida and changed his
address on his driver's license, his identification card/voter registration
application indicated that he was currently registered to vote, raising another serious issue. The fact that Mr. Zannie changed his address twice in
Florida and the driver license office file seemed to be current indicates that
his voter registration should have also reflected his change in address.
However, the driver license office failed to forward these address change
forms to the local supervisor of elections office despite Mr. Zannie's re-
peated requests.

Maria DeSoto, a poll worker in Palm Beach County, testified that
many eligible voters who registered through the DHSMV found their reg-
istrations were not transmitted to the supervisor of elections office. She
witnessed a couple that registered together at the DHSMV but only one
person's name was on the voter rolls on Election Day.[24]

The testimony of the witnesses who experienced problems voting after
they had applied with the Division of Driver Licenses seems to run counter to contentions made by Ms. Lambert that its motor voter registration
process is "very simple" and "very good." Despite some voters being

disenfranchised by failures in the motor voter process, the division never-theless maintains that it should not be blamed for the numbers of citizens who were deprived of their right to vote on Election Day.

ABSENTEE BALLOTS

At the Tallahassee hearing, **Alvin Peters**, an attorney from Panama City, testified that Governor Bush sent out a letter encouraging selected citizens to vote by mail. Mr. Peters claimed that this "vote by mail letter" offered selected citizens the opportunity to vote by mail, which is not allowed in Florida. He further pointed out the letter had the seal of the state of Florida and was signed by Governor Bush.[25]

Governor Bush disagreed with the above characterization of the letter referred to by Mr. Peters. He indicated to the Commission that the letter did not bear the current state seal, but rather the state seal as it first appeared in 1868.[26]

Following Mr. Peters' testimony and presentation of his supporting documents, **Moya Burgess** responded with outrage. She explained, "It makes me sick to think that . . . our governor basically sent out an infomercial to his party." She added that she is registered with "the other party" and she never received any information from the governor. In Ms. Burgess' opinion, this letter should have been addressed to all voters.[27]

POLICE PRESENCE AT OR NEAR POLLING SITES

Several Florida voters reported seeing Florida Highway Patrol (FHP) troopers in and around polling places. Troopers conducted an unauthorized vehicle checkpoint within a few miles of a polling place in a predomi-nantly African American neighborhood. In another area, trooper vehicles were reportedly parked within sight of at least two polling places, which one resident characterized as "unusual." The FHP reported that troopers only visited polling places to vote on Election Day. In light of the high voter turnout that was expected during the 2000 presidential election, par-ticularly among communities of color that may have a strained relation-ship with law enforcement, some Floridians questioned the timing of and the motivation for the FHP's actions.

Col. **Charles Hall**, director of the Florida Highway Patrol, testified at the Commission's Tallahassee hearing. He explained that the history of increased checkpoints by the FHP began in the early 1980s, when the ve-hicle inspection laws were repealed. The FHP determined that the most effective way to inspect a large number of vehicles was through driver's license/faulty vehicle equipment checkpoints. He also noted that he had no conversations with the office of the governor, the office of the attorney general, or the office of the secretary of state in preparation for the 2000 presidential election.

Colonel Hall admitted that on November 7, 2000, the FHP established a checkpoint on Oak Ridge Road in Southern Leon County between the hours of 10 A.M. and 11:30 A.M. The demographic makeup of the precincts surrounding the Oak Ridge Road checkpoint are as follows: (1) Precinct 107 is 82 percent Caucasian and 13 percent African American, (2) Precinct 109 is 37 percent Caucasian and 57 percent African American, and (3) Precinct 110 is 70 percent Caucasian and 24 percent African American.

Approximately 150 vehicles were stopped as a result of the Oak Ridge Road checkpoint that day. According to FHP records, of the sixteen citizens who received notices of faulty equipment, six (37 percent) were people of color.

On the afternoon of Election Day, the FHP received notice of a complaint to the attorney general's office that FHP troopers had hindered people of color from arriving at polling places due to the Oak Ridge Road checkpoint. Colonel Hall indicated that "the FHP was the first statewide law enforcement agency in the county to voluntarily begin collecting data concerning traffic stops in response to the racial profiling issue." The racial breakdown of the 150 drivers stopped at that checkpoint on Election Day, however, is not available.[28]

As a result of its investigation, the FHP found that some policy violations had occurred but concluded that no citizen was unreasonably delayed or prohibited from voting as a result of the Oak Ridge Road checkpoint. The policy violations cited by FHP's investigators included the fact that the checkpoint site was not on the monthly preapproved list and the media notification policy was not followed. The investigators recommended "counseling" for the sergeant in charge of the checkpoint and the district commander in charge of the media notification.

Colonel Hall stated the FHP was "very concerned about the perception people may have about what the patrol did that day." The Commission heard testimony from voters in Tallahassee regarding their reaction to the FHP's actions on Election Day. **Roberta Tucker**, an African American woman and a longtime resident of Tallahassee, was driving along Oak Ridge Road on her way to vote. Before Ms. Tucker could reach her polling place, she was stopped at an FHP vehicle checkpoint conducted by approximately five white troopers. According to Ms. Tucker, the checkpoint was located at the only main road leading to her assigned polling place. One of the troopers approached Ms. Tucker's car, asked for her driver's license, and after looking at it, returned it to her and allowed her to proceed. Ms. Tucker considered the trooper's actions to be "suspicious" because "nothing was checked, my lights, signals, or anything that [the state patrol] usually check." She also recalled being "curious" about the checkpoint because she had never seen a checkpoint at this location. Ms. Tucker added that she felt "intimidated" because "it was an Election Day and it was a big election and there were only white officers there and like I said, they didn't ask me for anything else, so I was suspicious at that."[29]

In response to the allegations of voter intimidation surrounding this checkpoint, Colonel Hall stated that "the checkpoint was properly conducted, and it was not anywhere near a polling facility, and I don't see how that could affect anybody's ability to vote." He added that he was "not really" surprised to learn that a trooper may have asked for a driver's license and not registration. He explained that such an action could occur if vehicles had begun to back up. Moreover, Colonel Hall stated he was "disappointed" that the FHP could not speak with Ms. Tucker because she refused to cooperate with their investigation. Ms. Tucker testified, however, that she reported the incident to her local NAACP and never returned the FHP's calls because "I felt it was a civil rights issue . . . I felt like it was sort of discriminatory."

When **John Nelson**, an African American resident of Jefferson County in Tallahassee, went to his assigned polling place, Precinct 6, to vote, he saw an unoccupied FHP vehicle parked across the street. He considered this to be "unusual" because he has voted a number of times at the same precinct but was not accustomed to seeing a law enforcement vehicle at the precinct. Moreover, Mr. Nelson stated he did not see any FHP troopers voting inside the precinct or leaving the precinct. Mr. Nelson added that his precinct is usually frequented by a large number of African American voters. The FHP vehicle's presence piqued Mr. Nelson's curiosity, and after voting, he drove to a precinct in the downtown area on North Washington Street and saw another FHP vehicle parked outside the precinct.[30]

In response to Mr. Nelson's allegations, Colonel Hall explained that those troopers only visited polling places to vote, and no parking tickets were written in the parking lots of voting precincts. He added that law enforcement personnel use a service station close to the polling place, which may have explained their presence. Furthermore, according to Colonel Hall, the FHP has "no policy that specifically excludes polling places from any law enforcement function." There is also no FHP policy against troopers wearing their uniforms or using their vehicles while voting at any election. At the request of supervisors of elections, the FHP has assisted in traffic control at polling places in the past, but the FHP received no such request for the November 2000 election.[31]

Florida Attorney General Robert A. Butterworth summarized his position on the use of law enforcement checkpoints on Election Day:

> What we do know is that a checkpoint on that date, Election Day, was absolutely not necessary for law enforcement purposes and similar

checkpoints should never again be implemented on Election Day . . .
No law enforcement barriers should be placed on Florida's road-
ways when people are going to and from voting.

Regardless of the motivation for the FHP's actions on Election Day, it
appears that a number of voters perceived, at minimum, that they were
negatively affected by the proximity of law enforcement officers to the
precincts around Tallahassee.[32]

VERIFIED TRANSCRIPT REFERENCES

1. Cathy Jackson, Testimony before the U.S. Commission on Civil
   Rights, Miami, FL, February 16, 2001, Verified Transcript, pp. 80–87.
   Ms. Jackson explained that her polling place's building was
   being used by two different "districts," which apparently refer to
   precincts. Ms. Jackson belonged to the first, whereas the elderly
   white voter belonged to the second.
2. Donnise DeSouza Testimony, Miami Verified Transcript, February
   16, 2001, pp. 54–58.
3. Angenora Ramsey Testimony, Miami Verified Transcript, February
   16, 2001, pp. 87–96.
4. Margarita Green Testimony, Miami Verified Transcript, February
   16, 2001, pp. 65–68. The supervisor of elections for Miami-Dade,
   however, provided a form signed by a Margarita C. Green pur-
   porting to indicate that she no longer lived in Miami-Dade
   County. Mrs. Green does not recall signing any such form. David
   Leahy, supervisor of elections, Miami-Dade County, letter to
   Edward A. Hailes, Jr., general counsel, U.S. Commission on Civil
   Rights, June 1, 2001, pp. 2–3.
5. R. Jai Howard, Testimony before the U.S. Commission on Civil
   Rights, Tallahassee, FL, January 11, 2001, Verified Transcript, p. 84.
   Florida A&M University houses a voting precinct on its campus.
6. Marilyn Nelson Testimony, poll worker, Precinct 232 in Miami-
   Dade County, Testimony, Miami Verified Transcript, February
   16, 2001, pp. 129–138.
7. Maria Desoto Testimony, Miami Verified Transcript, February
   16, 2001, p. 142.
8. Barbara Phoele Testimony, Miami Verified Transcript, February
   16, 2001, pp. 126–127, 136, 156. Ms. Phoele eventually posted the
   sign herself. Ibid., pp. 126–127.
9. Marvin Rickles, Jr., Testimony, Miami Verified Transcript, February
   16, 2001, p. 134.
10. Millard Suid Testimony, Miami Verified Transcript, February 16,
    2001, pp. 123, 132.

11. Randall Benston, precinct area chair, Precincts 6Z, 5Z, and 7B, Broward County, Testimony, Miami Verified Transcript, February 16, 2001, p. 457.

12. Lavonna Lewis Testimony, Miami Verified Transcript, February 16, 2001, pp. 102–106.

13. Donnise DeSouza Testimony, Miami Verified Transcript, February 16, 2001, pp. 54–56.

14. Susan Newman, affidavit submitted to U.S. Commission on Civil Rights, January 31, 2001, p. 3.

15. Millard Suid Testimony, Miami Verified Transcript, February 16, 2001, p. 123.

16. Robert Weisman, county administrator, Palm Beach County, Response to Commission's Interrogatory 1, April 11, 2001, p. 2.

17. Felix Boyle Testimony, Miami Verified Transcript, February 16, 2001, pp. 78–79, 90–91.

18. Curtis Gans Testimony, Tallahassee Verified Transcript, January 11, 2001, p. 135.

19. Maria Desoto, poll worker, Palm Beach County, Testimony, Miami Verified Transcript, February 16, 2001, p. 146.

20. Corrine Brown Testimony, Tallahassee Verified Transcript, January 12, 2001, p. 315.

21. Marcia Seamans Testimony, Miami Verified Transcript, February 16, 2001, pp. 110–13.

22. Sandra Lambert Testimony, Miami Verified Transcript, February 16, 2001, p. 231. Sandra Lambert Testimony, Miami Verified Transcript, February 16, 2001, pp. 173–75. Sandra Lambert, director, Division of Driver Licenses, letter to Edward A. Hailes, Jr., March 14, 2001, p. 1. The division has a disciplinary system for employees who violate requirements of the motor voter process. Records indicate that in the year 2000 two employees received counseling, six employees received oral reprimands, and one employee received a written reprimand regarding violations of agency procedures for the motor voter process.

23. Bill Zannie Testimony, Miami Verified Transcript, February 16, 2001, pp. 466–471.

24. Maria DeSoto Testimony, Miami Verified Transcript, February 16, 2001, p. 46.

25. Alvin Peters Testimony, Tallahassee Verified Transcript, January 12, 2001, p. 370.

26. See app. VI, Charles T. Canady, general counsel, Office of the Governor for the State of Florida, letter to Edward A. Hailes, Jr., June 6, 2001, p. 6.

27. Moya Burgess Testimony, Tallahassee Verified Transcript, January 12, 2001, p. 381.

28. Charles Hall Testimony, Tallahassee Verified Transcript, January 12, 2001, p. 119. Colonel Hall said, "Motorists who approach one of these checkpoints can expect to have their license, registration, insurance papers, tires, brake lights, and other safety equipment examined. And those with vehicles in good working order and have all their required paperwork normally will be delayed for less than a minute." In addition to the Oak Ridge Road checkpoint, the FHP established checkpoints in Bay and Escambia counties on November 7, 2000, pp. 178–179. Colonel Hall added that the district commander, Captain Speers, did a "post survey of [the area surrounding the checkpoint] and out of the 100 cars that he checked during that period of time, I believe it was 82 percent were white . . . 18 percent minority in that area," p. 179. Colonel Hall was unable to confirm if the conversation with the attorney general's office was memorialized in any way other than in the FHP's investigative report of the Oak Ridge Road checkpoint. According to Colonel Hall, the Oak Ridge Road checkpoint appeared on previous approved lists, but he did not believe the media notification procedures were avoided to prevent protests from civil rights organizations. Ibid., pp. 179–180. Colonel Hall further clarified that the counseling received by the troopers did not constitute a formal reprimand, p. 141.

29. Roberta Tucker Testimony, Tallahassee Verified Transcript, January 11, 2001, pp. 36–37.

30. John Nelson Testimony, Tallahassee Verified Transcript, January 11, 2001, pp. 26–27.

31. Ibid., p. 28. Mr. Nelson added that for the first time in his voting experience at his precinct, rather than simply showing his voter registration card, he was asked for two pieces of identification, which he considered to be "unusual." Ibid., p. 29.

32. Robert A. Butterworth Testimony, Tallahassee Verified Transcript, January 12, 2001, p. 199. Attorney General Butterworth also testified: "Therefore, I have prepared the legislation that I am forwarding to the Florida legislature that would prevent routine safety traffic checkpoints on Election Days anywhere within the state of Florida. There would be exceptions for roadblocks dictated by fleeing felons or other extreme circumstances."

Notes

INTRODUCTION

1. E. J. Dionne raises these concerns in this section in the thought provoking article, "When Did Voting Get so Intimidating?" *Washington Post*, October 31, 2004, B1.

2. Ibid.

3. Eric Fisher, "The Direct Recoding Electronic Voting Machine DRE Controversy," (Washington, DC: Congressional Research Service, 2005), 2.

CHAPTER 1

1. This section utilizes the work of Eric A. Fisher, "Voting Technologies in the United States: Overview and Issues for Congress" (CRS Report for Congress: Washington, DC), March 21, 2001.

2. Another form of early American voting was "voice vote" (calling out your vote before election clerks to be tallied) which was done before the 1890s. See Eric A Fisher, "Voting Technologies in the United States: Overview and Issues for Congress" (CRS Report for Congress: Washington, DC), March 21, 2001, p. 2.

3. Election Data Services, "2006 Voting Equipment Study," October 2, 2006, p. 3.

4. Ibid., 4.

5. Ibid., 2.

6. Ibid., 3.

7. Press Release, "Almost 55 Million, or One-Third of the Nations' Voters Will Face New Voting Equipment in 2006 Election," Election Data Services, October 2, 2006.

8. Election Data Services, "2006 Voting Equipment Study," October 2, 2006, 4.

9. Correspondents of the Washington Post, *Deadlock: The Inside Story of America's Closest Election* (New York: Public Affairs, 2001), 21. Also see E. J. Dionne, Jr., and William Kristol, *Bush v. Gore: The Court Cases and the Commentary* (Washington, DC:

Brookings Institution Press, 2001), 7. The six states where cases were litigated were California, Georgia, Illinois, New Mexico, Texas, and Florida.

10. These cases were filed the day after Election Day and were consolidated in *Fladell v. Palm Beach County Canvassing Board*, 772 So. 2d 1240 (Fla. 2000).

11. See Testimony of Kimball Brace, U.S. Commission on Civil Rights Hearings, Tallahassee transcript at 250–252, January 11, 2001; and Matt Bai and Michael Isikoff, "Clouds Over the Sunshine State," *Newsweek*, November 20, 2000, 16.

12. The U.S. Commission on Civil Rights, *Voting Irregularities in Florida During the 2000 Presidential Election*, 90. Each county supervisor of elections made a determination about the voting system the county would use from the list of voting technologies that were certified by the Florida secretary of state and the state Division of Elections. However, the county's budget played a significant role in the type of machines county supervisors of elections could select.

13. Josh Barbanel and Ford Fessenden, "Contesting the Vote," *New York Times*, November 29, 2000, A25.

14. See the U.S. Commission on Civil Rights, *Voting Irregularities in Florida During the 2000 Presidential Election* at http://www.usccr.gov/pubs/vote2000/report/ch8.htm#_ftn1. Also see the Florida Governors' Select Task Force, *Revitalizing Democracy in Florida*, 31–32.

15. See Testimony of Ion Sancho, U.S. Commission on Civil Rights Hearings, Tallahassee transcript at 17, January 12, 2001.

16. Ibid.

17. Ibid., 12–13.

18. The U.S. Commission on Civil Rights Reports, *Voting Irregularities*, 94.

19. Testimony of Jim Smith, U.S. Commission on Civil Rights Hearings, Tallahassee transcript at 166–167, January 11, 2001.

20. See Governor's Select Task Force, *Revitalizing Democracy in Florida*, 36. Florida's Governor, Jeb Bush, established the Select Task Force on Election Procedures, Standards, and Technology on December 14, 2000, to review the 2000 presidential election. The task force was comprised of ten Democrats, ten Republicans, and one independent. It held five meetings—January 8 and 9 in Tallahassee, January 23 in Orlando, February 1 in Davie near Fort Lauderdale, and February 6 in Jacksonville. The Select Task Force examined Florida's election procedures for about two months and presented its final report on March 1, 2001, to the governor, the president of the Florida Senate, the speaker of the House of Representatives, and the secretary of state. The final report focused on updating Florida's voting technology.

21. See Florida Legislature, Select Joint Committee on the Manner of Appointment of Presidential Electors, *Report and Recommendations* at 13, December 4, 2000. This aspect of the 2000 election fiasco is seldom discussed as well as the complications that would have risen if Florida had implemented the Legislature's decision to select its own slate of electors.

22. The only risks identified by the Joint Committee were that Congress would not count Florida's certified electors on November 26, 2000, if court cases were still pending on December 12, 2000, or if the election laws that determined the electors were changed from the laws of November 7, 2000. The Florida Legislature declared its authority to determine the manner of appointing electors is derived from Article II, Section 1 of the U.S. Constitution, and the 3 U.S. Code that it believed

granted state legislatures the power to appoint electors if the state missed its deadline. They also cited the U.S. Supreme Court case of *McPherson v. Blacker*, 146 U.S. 1 (1982) to justify the state legislature's "absolute power" to determine the state's electors. For the full report see Florida Legislature, Select Joint Committee on the Manner of Appointment of Presidential Electors, *Report and Recommendations*, December 4, 2000.

23. Kimball Brace, "Overview of Voting Equipment Usage in the United States," Statement to the United States Election Assistance Commission (Washington, DC: Election Data Services, May 5, 2004), 2.

24. The voting statistics in this section are the findings of the Election Data Services. See Election Data Services, "2006 Voting Equipment Study," October 2, 2006, p. 2. Kimball Brace, "Overview of Voting Equipment Usage in the United States," Statement to the United States Election Assistance Commission (Washington, DC: Election Data Services, May 5, 2004).

25. Steven F. Freeman and Joel Bleifuss, *Was the 2004 Presidential Election Stolen* (New York: Seven Stories Press, 2006), 58.

26. See "Raw Notes On: Voting Systems Organizations and Companies," January 14, 2005, http://www.thelandesreport.com/VotingMachineCompanies .htm. Last visited April 27, 2008. Also see http://www.ecotalk.org/VotingMachine Companies.htm.

27. Ibid.

28. Freeman and Bleifuss, *Was the 2004 Presidential Election Stolen*, 58.

29. http://www.thelandesreport.com/VotingMachineCompanies.htm.

30. Ibid.

31. Ibid.

32. Ibid. For further discussions also see Steven F. Freeman and Joel Bleifuss, *Was the 2004 Presidential Election Stolen* (New York: Seven Stories Press, 2006): 58, 59; and Beverly Harris, *Black Box Voting* (High Point, NC: Plan Nine Publishing, 2003).

CHAPTER 2

1. Valerie Jablow, "Lawsuit Cast Votes Against Electronic Voting Machine," *Trial*, August 1, 2006.

2. These are ongoing questions that have been raised by several election experts and voters. See http://www.votingmachinesprocon.org/questions/election06 .htm. Last visited April 27, 2008.

3. Ibid.

4. Ibid.

5. Abbe Waldman Delozier and Vickie Karp, *Hacked! High Tech Election Theft in America* (Austin, Texas: Truth Enterprises Publishing, 2006), 6.

6. Marcus Baram, "Poll Screw-Ups: Snow, Invisible Ink and Missing Ballots," February 5, 2008. See http://www.abcnews.go.com/Politics/story?id=4240895. Last visited February 12, 2008.

7. Ibid.

8. Deborah Hastings, "Primary Voters See Some Voting Hiccups," Associated Press, February 5, 2008.

9. Before the state could replace the machines there was a governor's recall election where it had to use the punch-card machines. The machines rejected many votes and significantly affected voters in Alameda, Los Angeles, Mendocino, Sacramento, San Bernardino, San Diego, Santa Clara, Shasta, and Solano.

10. See the Election Protection Coalition, "Shattering the Myth: An Initial Snapshot of Voter Disenfranchisement in 2004 Elections," December 2004 at http:// www.reformelections.org/research.asp?pubid=612.

11. Ibid.

12. Anna Kaplan, "Follow Nonexistent the Paper Trail: the Technological Advances in Electronic Voting Machines Rise Accountability Questions about Today's Democratic Process," *Humanist*, January/February 2005.

13. See the Election Protection Coalition, "Shattering the Myth: An Initial Snapshot of Voter Disenfranchisement in 2004 Elections" at http://www.reformelections .org/research.asp?pubid=612.

14. David Batstone, "Machine Ate My Vote," *Sojourners Magazine*, September 2004.

15. See http://www.votingmachinesprocon.org/questions/election06.htm.

16. David L. Dill, Bruce Schneier, and Barbara Simons, "Voting and Technology: Who Gets to Count Your Vote?" *Communications of the ACM* (Association for Computing Machinery), Vol. 46, No. 8, August 2003.

17. Waldman Delozier and Karp, *Hacked! High Tech Election Theft in America*, 29.

18. Ibid.

19. Baram, "Poll Screw-Ups: Snow, Invisible Ink and Missing Ballots."

20. See the report from Voters Unite at http://www.votersunite.org/MB2.pdf. Also see Election Protection at http://www.reformelections.org/research.asp?pubid=612.

21. Kaplan, "Follow Nonexistent the Paper Trail: the Technological Advances in Electronic Voting Machines Rise Accountability Questions About Today's Democratic Process."

22. See Bev Harris, *Black Box Voting: Ballot Tampering in the 21st Century* (High Point , NC: Plan Nine Publishing, 2003), 15.

23. The Election Protection Coalition is made up of national, state, and local organizations such as People For the American Way Foundation, Lawyers' Committee for Civil Rights Under Law, the National Coalition on Black Civic Participation, the Voter Protection Project of America's Families United, American Federation of Labor – Congress of Industrial Organizations, the National Association for the Advancement of Colored People, the Advancement Project, the NAACP Legal Defense & Educational Fund, the Mexican American Legal Defense and Educational Fund, the League of United Latin American Citizens, Unity '04, the National Bar Association, the National Council of La Raza, Labor Council for Latin American Advancement, Artists for a New South Africa, National Newspaper Publishers Association, National Association of Latino Elected and Appointed Officials, the American Civil Liberties Union, Working Assets, Project Vote, Common Cause, USAction, Center for Community Change, League of Women Voters, True Majority, Electronic Frontier Foundation, California Voter Fund, Verified Voting Foundation, Computer Professionals for Social Responsibility, the National Asian Pacific American Legal Consortium, the Gamaliel Foundation, the National Council of Churches, United Church of Christ, Unitarian Universalists, Union for Reform

Judaism, Jim Wallace of Sojourners Magazine/Call to Renewal, National Latina/o Law Students Association, VoteWatch, the Native American Rights Fund, the Leadership Conference on Civil Rights, the American Association of People with Disabilities, the Asian American Legal Defense and Education Fund, Rock the Vote, the National Congress of American Indians, the UniverSoul Circus, the National Black Law Students Association, IMPACT 2004, Just Democracy, Demos, the Brennan Center, the American Constitution Society, the Public Interest Research Group, the Southern Regional Council, and others.

24. See the report of the Election Protection Coalition at http://www.ep365 .org/site/c.fnKGIMNtEoG/b.2232255/k.AB55/Election_Protection_Update_1 .htm#ks. Last visited April 27, 2008.

25. "Election Reversed in Clay County . . . ," Associated Press in *Wichita Eagle*, August 22, 2002, 8B.

26. Election Protection Coalition, "Shattering the Myth: An Initial Snapshot of Voter Disenfranchisement in 2004 Elections."

27. See Harris, *Black Box Voting: Ballot Tampering in the 21st Century*, 31.

28. See the report of the Election Protection Coalition at http://www.ep365 .org/site/c.fnKGIMNtEoG/b.2232255/k.AB55/Election_Protection_Update_1 .htm#md.

29. Ibid.

30. Ibid.

31. Ibid.

32. Valerie Jablow, "Lawsuit Cast Votes Against Electronic Voting Machine," *Trial*, August 1, 2006.

33. Election Protection Coalition, "Shattering the Myth: An Initial Snapshot of Voter Disenfranchisement in 2004 Elections."

34. Ibid.

35. Ibid.

36. Ibid.

37. Ibid.

38. "Glitches Cause Delays for Morning Voters in Missouri," http://www.ksdk .com/news. Last visited February 5, 2008.

39. Baram, "Poll Screw-Ups: Snow, Invisible Ink and Missing Ballots."

40. Angela Delli Santi, "Questions Linger on Reliability of Electronic Voting in NJ," Associated Press, in *Courier-Post*, March 25, 2008.

41. See Harris, *Black Box Voting: Ballot Tampering in the 21st Century*, 30.

42. Election Protection Coalition, "Shattering the Myth: An Initial Snapshot of Voter Disenfranchisement in 2004 Elections."

43. Ibid.

44. Kaplan, "Follow Nonexistent the Paper Trail: the Technological Advances in Electronic Voting Machines Rise Accountability Questions About Today's Democratic Process." Also see http://www.verifiedvotingfoundation.org/article.php?li st=type&type=15#northcarolina.

45. Election Protection Coalition, "Shattering the Myth: An Initial Snapshot of Voter Disenfranchisement in 2004 Elections."

46. Sean Greene, "Voting Machine Vendors Face Rebuffs in States," *Campaign & Elections*, September 2005.

47. Batstone, "The Machine Ate My Vote."

48. See Harris, "Black Box Voting: Ballot Tampering in the 21st Century, 12.

49. See Waldman Delozier and Karp, *Hacked! High Tech Election Theft in America*, 202.

50. Mark Niquette, "Clinton, Obama Camp See Voting Problems," *Columbus Dispatch*, March 4, 2008.

51. *Moss v. Bush*, No. 04-2088-114.

52. Election Protection Coalition, "Shattering the Myth: An Initial Snapshot of Voter Disenfranchisement in 2004 Elections."

53. Anita Miller, ed., *What Went Wrong in Ohio* (Chicago, IL: Academy Publisher, 2005), 47.

54. Kaplan, "Follow Nonexistent the Paper Trail: the Technological Advances in Electronic Voting Machines Rise Accountability Questions About Today's Democratic Process."

55. Ibid.

56. Anita Miller, ed., *What Went Wrong in Ohio*, 49.

57. See the People for the American Way Foundation and the Election Protection Coalition election report, http://www.ep365.org/site/c.fnKGIMNtEoG/b.2232255/k.AB55/Election_Protection_Update_1.htm.

58. Election Protection Coalition, "Shattering the Myth: An Initial Snapshot of Voter Disenfranchisement in 2004 Elections."

59. Anita Miller, ed., *What Went Wrong in Ohio*, 64.

60. Ibid., 53.

61. Ibid., 55.

62. Steven Freeman and Joel Bleifuss, *Was the 2004 Presidential Election Stolen?* (New York: Seven Stories Press, 2006), 10.

63. See the People for the American Way Foundation and the Election Protection Coalition election report, at: http://www.ep365.org/site/c.fnKGIMNtEoG/b.2232255/k.AB55/Election_Protection_Update_1.htm.

64. Ibid.

65. Clive Thompson, "Can You Count on Voting Machines," *New York Times Magazine*, January 6, 2008.

66. See the People for the American Way Foundation and the Election Protection Coalition election report, http://www.ep365.org/site/c.fnKGIMNtEoG/b.2232255/k.AB55/Election_Protection_Update_1.htm.

67. Baram, "Poll Screw-Ups: Snow, Invisible Ink and Missing Ballots."

68. See Harris, *Black Box Voting: Ballot Tampering in the 21st Century*, 31.

69. Election Protection Coalition, "Shattering the Myth: An Initial Snapshot of Voter Disenfranchisement in 2004 Elections," p. 53.

70. "Ballot Glitches Reverse two Election Results," *Houston Chronicle*, November 8, 2002, A32.

71. See the People for the American Way Foundation and the Election Protection Coalition election report at http://www.ep365.org/site/c.fnKGIMNtEoG/b.2232255/k.AB55/Election_Protection_Update_1.htm#pa.

72. Election Protection Coalition, "Shattering the Myth: An Initial Snapshot of Voter Disenfranchisement in 2004 Elections," p. 53.

73. See Harris, *Black Box Voting: Ballot Tampering in the 21st Century*.

74. David L. Dill, Bruce Schneier, and Barbara Simons, "Voting and Technology: Who Gets to Count Your Vote?" *Communications of the ACM* (Association for Computing Machinery), Vol. 46, No. 8, August 2003.

75. *Reynolds v. Sims*, 377 U.S. 533, 555 (1964).

CHAPTER 3

1. See similar questions in Eric Fisher's, "The Direct Recording Electronic Voting Machine" (Washington, DC: Congressional Research Service, December 14, 2005).

2. Ibid., 4.

3. Ibid.

4. Clive Thompson, "Can You Count on Voting Machines," *New York Time Magazine*, January 6, 2008.

5. Eric Fisher, "Voting Technologies in the United States: Overview and Issues for Congress" (Washington, DC: Congressional Research Service, March 21, 2001), 9.

6. See Aviel Rubin, *Brave New Ballot* (New York: Morgan Books, 2006), 2–3.

7. Tadayoshi Kohno, Adam Stubblefield, Aviel Rubin, and Dan S. Wallach, "Analysis of an Electronic Voting System," John Hopkins University Information Security Report, February 27, 2004. http://avirubin.com/vote/analysis/.

8. Ibid.

9. Ibid.

10. Peter Piazza, "Keeping the Vote In," *Security Management*, April 1, 2004.

11. Ibid.

12. Alec Yasinsac, David Wagner, Matt Bishop, Ted Baker, Breno de Medeiros, Gary Tyson, Michael Shamos, and Mike Burmester, "Software Review and Security Analysis of the ES&S iVotronic 8.0.1.2 Voting Machine Firmware, Final Report to the Florida Department of State" (Tallahassee, FL: Security and Assurance in Information Technology Laboratory, Florida State University), February 23, 2007.

13. *Deseret Morning News*, "Doubts Swirl on Security of Electronic Voting," January 7, 2008.

14. Ariel J. Feldman, J. Alex Halderman, and Edward W. Felten, "Security Analysis for the Diebold AccuVote-TS Voting Machine," Center for Information Technology Policy: Princeton University, 2006.

15. David L. Dill, Bruce Schneier, and Barbara Simons, "Voting and Technology: Who Gets to Count Your Vote?" *Communications of the ACM*, Vol. 46, No. 8, August 2003. Also see Rubin, *Brave New Ballot*, 14, and see http://www.verifiedvoting foundation.org/article.php?id=5028.

16. National Institute of Standards & Technology Study, "Requiring Software Independence in VVSG 2007: STS Recommendations for the TGDC," November 2006.

17. Ibid.

18. Ibid.

19. Cameron W. Barr, "Security of Electronic Voting is Condemned," *Washington Post*, December 1, 2006, A01.

20. Ibid.

21. Dill, Schneier, and Simons, "Voting and Technology: Who Gets to Count Your Vote?"

22. Ibid.

23. Thompson, "Can You Count on Voting Machines."

24. See http://www.votersunite.org/info/needsolutionarticles.asp.

25. Adam Cohen, "The Good News (Really) About Voting Machines," *New York Times*, January 10, 2007.

26. Reprint by permission from http://www.verifiedvoting.org. Last visited October 3, 2008.

27. See Election Science Institute, "DRE Analysis for May 2006 Primary, Cuyahoga County, Ohio," August 2006.

28. Thompson, "Can You Count on Voting Machines."

29. Dill, Schneier, and Simons, "Voting and Technology: Who Gets to Count Your Vote?"

30. Ibid.

31. Thompson, "Can You Count on Voting Machines."

32. Adam Cohen, "The Good News (Really) About Voting Machines," *New York Times*, January 10, 2007.

33. Thompson, "Can You Count on Voting Machines."

34. See similar questions raised by Kevin Shelly, former California Secretary of State, "Address before the Voting Systems Panel on the Results the Diebold Election Systems audit installed in 17 California counties," 2003. Available at http://www.verifiedvoting.org/article.php?id=5021. Last visited February 10, 2008.

CHAPTER 4

1. See Tom Joyner, Testimony, U.S. House of Representative, Committee on House Administration, April 9, 2008.

2. As of the time of this writing, forty-three states had held primaries. But additional primaries will occur after the press time of this book, and therefore the number of states reporting voting complaints may increase.

3. See http://www.ncffe.org/2008PrimariesReport. Also see the Election Protection Coalition report of voting problems in 2006 at http://www.EP365.org.

4. The following testimonies are quoted from Bob Fitrakis and Harvey Wasserman, "Hearings on Ohio Voting Put 2004 Election in Doubt," *Columbus Free Press,* November 18, 2004. Reprinted with permission.

5. Election Protection Coalition, "Shattering the Myth: An Initial Snapshot of Voter Disenfranchisement in 2004 Elections," December 2004. http://www.reformelections.org/research.asp?pubid=612.

6. Anita Miller, ed., *What Went Wrong in Ohio: The Conyers Report on the 2004 Presidential Election* (Chicago: Academy Chicago Publishers, 2005), 4–5.

7. Ibid., 3.

8. Ibid., 5, 6.

9. Doug Gross, "Group Finds Voting Irregularities in South," Associated Press, November 5, 2004.

10. See DeWayne Wickham, "The Press Missed a Critical Post-Election Day Story in Florida," *Nieman Reports* 55, no. 1 (Spring 2001), 78. See David Firestone, "Drive Under Way to Raise Turnout of Black Voters," *New York Times*, October 29,

2000, A1. See Michael A. Fletcher, "In Targeted States, A Striking Turnout of Black Voters," *Washington Post*, November 17, 2000, A29.

11. The complaints included *Horowitz v. Lepore*, No. 00-10970 (15th Jud. Cir., Palm Beach County, Nov. 9, 2000); *Elkin v. Lepore*, No. 00-10988 AE (15th Jud. Cir., Palm Beach County, Nov. 9, 2000); *Haitian American Bureau and Int'l Liaison v. Palm Beach County Board*, No. 00-11084-AH (15th Jud. Cir., Palm Beach County, Nov 9, 2000); *Gibbs v. Palm Beach County Board*, No. 00-11D00-AH (15th Jud. Cir., Palm Beach County, Nov 9, 2000); *Brown v. Staffard*, No-00-2878 (2nd Judicial Cir., Leon County, Dec. 5, 2000); *Roger v. Election Canvassing Commission of Florida*, No. 00-109922-AF (15th Jud. Cir., Palm Beach County, Nov. 9, 2000); *Crum v. Palm Beach County Canvassing Board*, No. 00-11029-AI (15th Jud. Cir., Palm Beach County, Dec. 1, 2000); *Litchman v. Bush*, No: CL-00-11098 (15th Jud. Cir., Palm Beach County, Nov. 13, 2000); *Gottfried v. LePore*, No: CL-00-11091-AN (Fla. Sup. Ct., Palm Beach County, Nov. 13, 2000); and *Katz v. Florida Election Canvassing Board*, No. CL-00-11302-AB (15th Jud. Cir., Palm Beach County, Nov. 17, 2000).

12. Florida was not the only state with complaints of voting irregularities. In Illinois, many voters that registered at motor vehicle bureaus were informed on Election Day that they were not on the voter registration list and could not vote. In Cleveland, thousands of voters were unable to cast a ballot because their polling places moved without notice. There were similar patterns reported in St. Louis and Chicago.

13. These organizations included: The Puerto Rican Legal Defense and Education Fund in New York City that received complaints from their constituents in Florida from thousands of Latino voters who were prevented from voting; The Association of Indians in America and the South Florida chapter of the Organization of Chinese Americans reported that East Indians and Asians were unable to vote in Florida; and the NAACP received complaints in their Baltimore, Maryland, national office and sent 200 volunteers throughout the state of Florida to observe irregularities and assist voters. See the U.S. Commission on Civil Rights Report, *Voting Irregularities in Florida During the 2000 Presidential Election* (Washington, DC: U.S. Government Printing Office, 2001), 6.

14. See the U.S. Commission on Civil Rights Report, *Voting Irregularities in Florida During the 2000 Presidential Election*.

15. See "Law and Justice," *Jet*, June 10, 2002, 36.

16. See Testimony of Donnise Desouza, NAACP Public Hearing, Miami Verified Transcript Vol. II at 52–56, November 11, 2000.

17. See Testimony of Andree Berwotiz, NAACP Public Hearing, Miami Verified Transcript Vol. III at 13–14, November 11, 2000.

18. See Testimony of Dymon Raimer, NAACP Public Hearing, Miami Verified Transcript Vol. II at 45, November 11, 2000.

19. See Testimony of Katreece Dunbar, NAACP Public Hearing, Miami Verified Transcript Vol. III at 23–24, November 11, 2000.

20. See *NAACP v. Harris*, No. 01-CIV-120-GOLD (Fla. Dist. Ct., Jan. 10, 2001).

21. The members of the Commission during the 2000 investigation were as follows: Mary Frances Berry—*Chairperson*, Cruz Reynoso—*Vice Chairperson*, Christopher Edley, Jr., Yvonne Y. Lee, Elsie M. Meeks, Russell G. Redenbaugh, Abigail Thernstrom, and Victoria Wilson.

22. Witnesses subpoenaed were: Florida Governor Jeb Bush; Florida Secretary of State Katherine Harris; members of Governor Bush's Select Task Force on Election Procedures, Standards and Technology; Florida's attorney general; state officials responsible for oversight of motor voter registration; the general counsel for Florida's Elections Commission; the director of the Division of Elections; the director of Florida's Highway Patrol; local elections officials; county supervisors; poll workers; local sheriffs; and Database Technologies (the company contracted to remove felons statewide from Florida's voter registration lists).

23. See U.S. Commission on Civil Rights, *Voting Irregularities in Florida during the 2000 Presidential Election*, 28.

24. Testimony of Maria Desoto, U.S. Commission on Civil Rights Hearings, Miami Transcript at 146–147, February 16, 2001.

25. See U.S. Commission on Civil Rights, *Voting Irregularities in Florida during the 2000 Presidential Election.*

26. See U.S Commission on Civil Rights, *Election Reform: An Analysis of Proposals and the Commission's Recommendations for Improving America's Election System* (U.S. Government Printing Office: Washington, DC, 2001). Other sources that have published strategies for election reform that mainly focus on updating Florida's election technology include Florida's Governor Select Task Force on Election Procedures, Standards, and Technology; The Constitution Project; and the Florida Justice Institute and the ACLU of Florida. Congress also enacted H.R. 3295, the "Help America Vote Act of 2002," to address election reform.

27. Ibid., iii.

28. The Commission is an investigative body cannot hold trials, give a ruling, or determine liabilities. It can however, initiate the litigation process or request remedies to redress violations.

29. U.S. Commission on Civil Rights, *Voting Irregularities in Florida During the 2000 Presidential Election*, xii.

30. Ibid. Also see Spencer Overton, "A Place at the Table: Bush v. Gore Through the Lens of Race," *Florida State University Law Review* 29, no. 2 (Fall 2001), 469.

31. Laura Parker and Peter Eisler, "Ballots in Black Florida Precincts Invalidated More," *USA Today*, April 6, 2001, A1.

32. John Mintz and Dan Keating, "Florida Ballots Spoilage Likelier for Blacks," *The Washington Post*, December 3, 2000, p. A1.

33. Ibid.

34. Ibid.

35. U.S. Commission on Civil Rights, *Voting Irregularities in Florida during the 2000 Presidential Election*, xii.

36. Ibid., 53.

37. See Governors' Task Force, *Revitalizing Democracy*, 31–32.

38. U.S. Commission on Civil Rights, *Voting Irregularities in Florida during the 2000 Presidential Election*, xii.

39. *Stewart v. Blackwell*, 444 F.3d 843 (6th Cir. 2006).

40. *Wexler v. Florida* Case No: SC04-1844.

41. *White v. Blackwell*, No. 3:05CV7309 (N.D. Ohio filed Dec. 8, 2005).

42. *ACLU v. Brunner*, Case 1:08-cv-00145 (filed 1/17/08); *ACORN v. Bysiewicz*, Case 3:04-cv-01624-MRK (D. Conn filed, September 28, 2004); *NAMUDNO v. Gonzales*,

Northwest Austin Mun. Util Dist. No.1 (*NAMUDNO v. Gonzales*) No. 1:06-cv-01284-PLF (D.D.C. August 4, 2006); *NAMUDNO v. Mukasey*, ____F. Supp.2d___, 2008 WL 2221034 (D.D.C. May 30, 2008); *Gooden v. Worley*, Case 2:05-cv- 02562-WMA (N.D. Ala.) CJ-AL-0003(filed May 26, 2006).

43. Voting Rights Act, 42 U.S.C. §1971 (a)(2)(A)[emphasis added].

44. U.S. Commission on Civil Rights, *Voting Irregularities in Florida*, 55.

45. See U.S. Commission on Civil Rights, *Voting: 1961 Commission on Civil Rights Report* (Washington, DC: U.S. Government Printing Office, 1961); U.S. Commission on Civil Rights, *The Voting Rights Act: Unfilled Goals* (Washington, DC: U.S. Government Printing Office, 1981).

46. Barbara Y. Phillips, *How to Use Section 5 of the Voting Rights Act* 3rd ed., (Washington, DC: Joint Center for Political Studies, 1983).

47. Ibid., 12–13; and Langlin McDonald, "The Quite Revolution in Minority Voting Rights," *Vanderbilt Law Review* 51 (Fall 1983), 1249–1297.

48. Lani Guinier, "And to the C Student: The Lessons of Bush v. Gore," in Ronald Dworkin, ed., *A Badly Flawed Election* (New York: The New Press, 2002), 249.

49. *Wesberry v. Sanders*, 376 U.S.1, 17 (1964).

CHAPTER 5

1. Richard L. Hasen, "Fraud Reform? How Efforts to ID Voting Problems Have Become a Partisan Mess," http://www.slate.com, posted February 22, 2006.

2. See the National Clean Elections Lawsuit, *Robert L. Schulz, et al v. State of New York, et al.* (Case No. 07-943).

3. Press Release, "50 States Sued to Block Computerized Vote Counting," We the People Foundation for Constitutional Education, New York, November 6, 2007.

4. *ACLU v. Brunner* filed against Ohio Secretary of State Jennifer Brunner, the Cuyahoga County Board of Commissioners, and the Cuyahoga County Board of Elections.

5. ACLU Press Release, "ACLU Challenges Ohio's Unequal Voting Technology in Federal Court," January 17, 2008.

6. Ibid.

7. Ibid.

8. *Stewart v. Blackwell*, 444 F.3d 843 (6th Cir. 2006).

9. See Section 512(f) of the Digital Millennium Copyright Act and *Online Policy Group v. Diebold*, 337 F.Supp.2d 1195.

10. MD Code, Election Law § 9-102(c)(1) (emphasis added).

11. *Online Policy Group v. Diebold*, 337 F.Supp.2d 1195.

12. Ibid.

13. See Section 512(f) of the Digital Millennium Copyright Act and *Online Policy Group v. Diebold*.

14. *Wirth v. Election Systems and Software* (ES&S) Inc., No. 01-MR-6 (2001).

15. *Holder v. McPherson*, No. CV 06-02923 SBA (Cal., San Francisco County Super. Ct. filed Mar. 21, 2006).

16. Plaintiffs included Riverside County Board of Supervisors was joined by Kern and Plumas counties and San Bernardino County and disabled rights advocates.

17. *National Federation of the Blind v. Volusia County*, Case No. 05-13990-B.

18. *Chavez v. Brewer*, No. CV 2006-007000 (Ariz., Maricopa County Super. Ct. filed May 9, 2006).

19. *Conroy v. Dennis* No. 06CV (CO, Denver County Dist. Ct. filed June 1, 2006).

20. The NAACP and ACLU filed the suit for Indiana legislator William Crawford, who represents the state's poorest districts in *Crawford v. Marion County Election Board*, No. 07-21. The other case was *Indiana Democratic Party v. Rokita*, No. 07-25, against Indiana's Secretary of State Todd Rokita, in his official capacity.

21. *Crawford v. Marion County Election Board*, No. 07-21 and *Indiana Democratic Party v. Rokita*, No. 07-25.

22. Linda Greenhouse, "Justices Agree to Hear Case about Voter ID Laws" *New York Times*, September 26, 2007.

23. Ibid.

24. Brenda Goodman, "Judge Blocks Requirement in Georgia for Voter ID," *New York Times*, July 6, 2006. See http://www.nytimes.com/2006/07/08/us/08voter.html.

25. See Stacy Forster, "State Legislature Consider Voter ID Amendment Advances," *Journal Sentinel*, November 1, 2005.

26. Plaintiffs were the Washington Citizen Action, Washington Association of Churches, the Washington Association of Community Organizations for Reform Now (ACORN), the Chinese Information and Service Center, the Service Employees International Union, Local 775 (SEIU), the Filipino American Political Action Group of Washington, the Organization of Chinese Americans (Greater Seattle Chapter), and the Korean American Voters Alliance.

27. *Washington Association of Churches v. Reed*, No.CV06-0726 RSM.

28. Suit was filed by the Southwest Voter Registration, NAACP's Florida chapter, Education Project and the Haitian-American Grassroots Coalition.

29. See http://www.brennancenter.org/content/resource/florida_naacp_v_browning.

30. Plaintiffs included Project Vote, People for the American Way, Common Cause Ohio, Foundation Association of Community Organizers for Reform Now, and Communities of Faith Assemblies Church.

31. See *Project Vote v. Blackwell*, No. 1:06 cv 1628.

32. *League of Women Voters of Florida v. Cobb*, 447 F. Supp. 2d 1314 (S.D. Fla. 2006).

33. The plaintiffs were League of Women Voters of Florida, People Acting for Community Together (PACT), community organizations, churches, synagogues and schools in Miami-Dade County, American Federation of State, County and Municipal Employees, Council 79 (AFSCME), and Service Employees International Union-Florida Healthcare Union (SEIU-FHU).

34. *Gonzalez v. Arizona*, No. cv06-1268.

35. *Purcell v. Gonzalez*, 127 S.Ct. 5 (2006).

36. *Boustani v. Blackwell*, No. 1:06CV2065.

37. Eric A. Fisher, "The Direct Recording Electronic Voting Machines: Controversy: FAQs and Misperceptions" (Washington, DC: CRS Report for Congress), September 26, 2006.

38. *State of Ohio and The People for the American Way Foundation v. Kenneth Blackwell and the Cuyahoga County Board of Elections*, No.CA 04 085597.

39. *Schering v. Blackwell* in U.S. District Court, Case No. 1:04-cv-755.

40. Ohio statute R.C. §3501.05.

41. *Gusciora v. McGreevey*, No. A-002842-04T1, 2006WL 1765061 (NJ. Super. Ct. App. Div., June 29, 2006).

CHAPTER 6

1. Lee Epstein and Thomas Walker, *Constitutional Law in a Changing America: Institutional Powers and* Constraints (Washington, DC: CQ Press, 2001), 57.

2. E.J. Dionne raises the concerns in this section in the thought provoking article, "When Did Voting Get so Intimidating?" *Washington, Post*, October 31, 2004, B1.

3. The vast majority of the studies on Federalism do not fully explore the interaction between state courts and the Supreme Court as an aspect of Federalism. Mainstream literature on Federalism focuses on the interaction between Congress, the president, and the states. There is an abundance of literature on the subject. See works on federalism such as Daniel J. Elazar, *Exploring Federalism* (Tuscaloosa: The University of Alabama Press, 1987); Alpheus Thomas Mason, ed., *The States' Rights Debate: Antifederalism and the Constitution* (New York: Oxford University Press, 1972); Raoul Berger, *Federalism* (Norman: University of Oklahoma Press, 1987); Aaron Wildavsky, *American Federalism in Perspective* (Boston: Little, Brown and Company, 1967); and Randy E. Barnett, ed., *The Rights Retained by the People* (Fairfax, VA: George Mason University Press, 1989). For a classic statement on federalism see M. J. C. Vile, *The Structure of American Federalism* (London: Oxford University Press, 1961); Daniel Elazar, *American Federalism: A View from the States* (New York: Crowell, 1972); and V. O. Key, Jr., *Southern Politics in State and Nation* (Knoxville: University of Tennessee Press, 1984).

4. One scholar observed, "That conclusion seems to turn federalism principles on their head and foretells an increased role for the Supreme Court in subsequent disputes over the interpretation and application of state law." See Harold J. Krent, "Judging Judging: The Problem of Second-Guessing State Judges' Interpretation of State Law in Bush v. Gore," *Florida State University Law Review* 29, no. 2 (Fall 2001), 494.

5. See generally Gordon S. Wood, *The Creation of the American Republic 1776–1787* (Chapel Hill: University of North Carolina Press, 1969). Also see Daniel A. Farber and Suzanna Sherry, *A History of the American Constitution* (St. Paul, MN: West Publishing, 1990).

6. *United States v. Lopez*, 514 U.S. 549, 576 (1995). For a classic statement on federalism see M. J. C. Vile, *The Structure of American Federalism* (London: Oxford University Press, 1961); Daniel Elazar, *American Federalism: A View from the States* (New York: Crowell, 1972); and V. O. Key, Jr., *Southern Politics in State and Nation* (Knoxville: University of Tennessee Press, 1984).

7. John R. Schmidhauser, "States' Rights and the Origin of the Supreme Court's power as Arbiter in Federal-State Relations," *Wayne Law Review* 4, no. 2 (Spring 1958), 111. Federalism was shaped out of a compromise between federalist and states' rights advocates. See discussions by Carl J. Friedrich, *Trends of Federalism in Theory and Practice* (New York: Praeger Publishers, 1968): 11; Martin Diamond, "What the Framers Meant by Federalism," and "The Federalist's View of Federalism," in

As Far as Republican Principles Will Admit: Essays by Martin Diamond, William A. Schambra, ed. (Washington, DC: AEI Press, 1992): 93–107, 108–143; Rufus S. Davis, *The Federal Principle: A Journey Through Time in Quest of a Meaning* (Berkeley: University of California Press, 1978): 74–120; and generally Samuel Beer, *To Make a Nation: The Rediscovery of American Federalism* (Cambridge, Mass.: Belknap Press, 1993).

8. Jacob E. Cooke, *The Federalist* (Middletown, CT: Wesleyan University Press, 1961), 553. For a discussion on how our system evolved see David A. Logan, "Judicial Federalism in the Court of History," *Oregon Law Review* 66, no. 3 (Fall 1988); and Lee Epstein and Thomas Walker, *Constitutional Law in a Changing America: Institutional Powers and Constraints* (Washington, DC: CQ Press, 2001).

9. Sheldon Goldman, *Constitution Law*, 2nd edition (New York: Harper Collins Publishers, 1991), 26. Also see Justice Breyer's dissent, *Bush v. Gore*, 531 U.S. 98, 144 (2000).

10. *Herb v. Pitcairn*, 324 U.S. 117, 125–126 (1945).

11. *Michigan v. Long*, 463 U.S 1032, 1041 (1983). Also see discussion on the impact of the case by Harold Krent, "Judging Judging: The Problem of Second-Guessing State Judges' Interpretation of State Law in Bush v. Gore" *Florida State University Law Review* 29, no. 2 (Fall 2001): 530–533; and Peter Shane, "Disappearing Demcoracy: How Bush v. Gore Undermined the Federal Right to Vote for Presidential Electors," *Florida State University Law Review* 29, no. 2 (Fall 2001): 537, 581–584.

12. Ibid.

13. Ibid., 1040.

14. See generally William J. Brennan, "The Bill of Rights and the States: The Revival of State Constitutions as Guardians of Individual Rights," *New York University Law Review* 61, no. 4 (1986), 535–553.

15. Harold J. Spaeth, "Burger Court Review of State Court Civil Liberties Decisions," *Judicature* 68, no. 7 (1985), 285.

16. William Brennan, "State Constitutions and the Protection of Individual Liberties," *Harvard Law Review* 90, no. 3 (1977), 502.

17. Ibid.

18. Shirley S. Abrahamson and Diane S. Gutman, "The New Judicial Federalism: State Constitutions and State Court," 97.

19. For contributions to the body of literature on judicial federalism see G. Alan Tarr, *State Constitutional Politics: An Historical Perspective in Constitutional Politics in the State* (Westport, CT: Greenwood Press, 1996); Donald J. Farole, Jr., *Interest Groups and Judicial Federalism: Organizational Litigation in State Judiciaries* (Westport, CT: Praeger, 1998); and Michael E. Solimne and James L. Walker, *Respecting State Court: The Inevitability of Judicial Federalism* (Westport, CT: Greenwood Press, 1999).

20. Michael E. Solimne and James L. Walker, *Respecting State Court: The Inevitability of Judicial Federalism*, 4. Also see works such as Shirley S. Abrahamson and Diane S. Guttmann, "New Federalism: State Constitutions and State Courts," in Burke Marshall, ed., *A Workable Government: The Constitution after 200 Years* (New York: W.W. Norton & Company, 1987); and "The New Judicial Federalism: State Constitutions and State Court," *Judicature* 71, no. 2 (1987).

21. Ibid., 97.

22. *Palm Beach County Canvassing Board v. Harris*, 772 So. 2d 1220, 1227-40 (2000).

23. Ibid.

24. *Bush v. Gore*, 531 U.S. 98, 138 (2000). She cited cases such as *Chevron U.S.A. Inc. v. Natural Resources Defense Council, Inc.*, 467 U.S. 837 (1984); *Stone v. Powell*, 428 U.S. 465 (1976); and *O'Dell v. Netherlands*, 521 U.S. 151 (1997). See the special *Bush v. Gore* edition of Florida State University Law Review for various scholars' discussion on the subject, *Florida State University Law Review* 29, no. 2 (Fall 2001).

25. *Bush v. Gore*, 531 U.S. 98, 137 (Ginsburg, J., dissenting) (2000).

26. *Bush v. Gore*, 531 U.S. 98, 139 (Ginsburg, J., dissenting) (2000).

27. Ibid., 112.

28. The principal precedents cited were *Bouie v. City of Columbia*, 378 U.S. 347 (1964); *NAACP v. Alabama ex rel. Patterson*, 357 U.S. 449 (1958); and *Fairfax's Devisee v. Hunter's Lessee*, 7 Cranch 603 (1813).

29. *Bush v. Gore*, 531 U.S. 98, 141 (Ginsburg, J., dissenting) (2000).

30. See Harold J. Krent, "Judging Judging: The Problem of Second-Guessing State Judges' Interpretation of State Law in Bush v. Gore," *Florida State University Law Review* 29, no. 2 (Fall 2001), 493–494.

31. The works of various scholars is utilized in this section such as J.W. Allen, *A History of Political Thought in the Sixteenth Century* (London: Methuen, 1957); Philip B. Kurland and Ralph Lerner, *The Founders' Constitution: Major Themes* vol. 1 (Chicago: University of Chicago Press, 1987); and William B. Gwyn, *The Meaning of the Separation of Powers* (New Orleans, LA: Tulane University Press, 1965). See generally Charles de Secondat Baron de Montesquieu, *The Spirit of Laws* (Amherst, NY: Prometheus Books, 2002).

32. M. J. C. Vile, *Constitutionalism and the Separation of Powers* (Oxford: Clarendon Press, 1967), 23–25.

33. Political theorists such as Marchamont Nedham, Sir William Blackstone, James Harrington, John Locke, George Lawson, Charles de Montesquieu, Jean Bodin, Plato, and Aristotle are some of the early writers of the separation of powers doctrine.

34. Many scholars share this view. For example, see William B. Gwyn, *The Meaning of the Separation of Powers* (New Orleans, La.: Tulane University Press, 1965). See generally Charles de Secondat Baron de Montesquieu, *The Spirit of Laws* (Amherst, NY: Prometheus Books, 2002); and M. J. C. Vile, *Constitutionalism and the Separation of Powers* (Oxford: Clarendon Press, 1967).

35. See generally Charles de Secondat Baron de Montesquieu, *The Spirit of Laws*.

36. Ibid., 152.

37. Ibid., 150.

38. Ibid., 152.

39. See the works of Philip B. Kurland and Ralph Lerner, *The Founders' Constitution: Major Themes* Vol. 1 (Chicago: University of Chicago Press, 1987); W. Allen, *A History of Political Thought in the Sixteenth Century* (London: Methuen, 1957); J. G. A. Pocock, *The Political Work of James Harrington* (New York: Cambridge University Press, 1977); and William B. Gwyn, *The Meaning of the Separation of Powers* (Tulane University, 1965).

40. For classic statements on separation of powers see William B. Gwyn, *The Meaning of the Separation of Powers* (Tulane University, 1965); Arthur T. Vanderbilt, *The Doctrine of the Separation of Powers and Its Present Day Significance* (Lincoln: University of Nebraska Press, 1953); M. J. C. Vile, *Constitutionalism and the Separation of*

Powers (Oxford: Clarendon Press, 1967); and Barbara B. Knight, *Separation of Powers in the American Political System* (Fairfax, VA: George Mason University Press, 1989).

41. Jacob E. Cooke, *The Federalist* (Middletown, CT: Wesleyan University Press, 1961), 349.

42. Ibid., 351.

43. Articles I, II, and III of the United States Constitution states in part: Article I—all legislative powers shall be vested in a Congress of the United States to the extent that they are granted to the federal state by the Constitution; Article II—that the executive power of the federal states shall be vested in the president of the United States; Article III—all the judicial power of the federation shall be vested in one supreme court and in such inferior courts as the Congress shall establish.

44. Article III provides: "The judicial power shall extend to all cases, in law and equity, arising under this Constitution, the laws of the United States, and Treaties made, or which shall be made, under their Authority. Section 2, cl. 2 states, "In all Cases affecting Ambassadors, other public Ministers and Consuls, and those in which a State shall be a Party, the Supreme Court shall have original Jurisdiction." See the United States Constitution, Article III.

45. Stephen Elliot, ed., *A Reference Guide to the United States Supreme Court* (New York: Sachem Publishing Associates, Inc., 1986), 28–33. He discussed that these three major judicial limitations are defined as: Jurisdiction—Article III, section 2 defines the Court's jurisdiction, whether a federal or state court has the authority to hear a case. Standing—Only the appropriate person/s can bring the case to the courts. Article III requires the plaintiff to have standing. "This means a plaintiff cannot raise another person's legal rights; plaintiff must show personal injury; injuries cannot be speculative; injuries must be traceable to the complaint, the laws must protect the grievance; and a relief from the injury must be possible." Justiciability—The case must be appropriate for court to make a decision.

46. Ibid., 32–33, 65–68.

47. Ibid. These terms are defined as follows: Ripeness—the issues are still developing and therefore not ready for the courts to review the issue; Mootness—the question is old and therefore a judiciary's intervention would not be necessary; Political Question—issues that are political in nature and another branch of government may have the authority to hear and resolve the matter; and Advisory Opinion—courts cannot be requested to render an opinion about a legal question, there must be an actual dispute between the parties.

48. For a discussion on the doctrine see generally Philippa Strum, *The Supreme Court and Political Questions* (Tuscaloosa: University of Alabama Press, 1974), Sanford Levison and Ernest Young, "Who's Afraid of the Twelfth Amendment?" *Florida State University Law Review* 29, no. 2 (Fall 2001): 968; and Harold Krent, "Judging Judging: The Problem of second Guessing State Judges' Interpretation of State Law In Bush v. Gore," *Florida State University Law Review* 29, no. 2 (Fall 2001): 510.

49. The residents made a proposal to the state government to change the requirements, which was rejected. The government placed the state under martial law when the residents created their own government. It feared the residents would support the new constitution. After the government regained control, Martin Luther, a resident sued and claimed the Rhode Island Charter violated Article IV, Section 4 of the U.S. Constitution. He asked the court to declare the charter

government illegitimate and to replace it with the new constitution. See *Luther v. Borden*, 7 Howard 1 (1849).

50. *Colegrove v. Green* 328 U.S. 549, 556 (1946).

51. *Baker v. Carr*, 369 U.S. 186, 217 (1962). For more analysis on this case as it relates to *Bush v. Gore* see Robert J. Pushaw, Jr., "The Presidential Election Dispute, The Political Question Doctrine, and the Fourteenth Amendment: A Reply to Professors Krent and Shane," *Florida State University Law Review* 29, no. 2 (Fall 2001), 611.

52. *Goldwater v. Carter*, 444 U.S. 996, 1003 (1979). This case involved President Jimmy Carter's termination of a U.S. treaty with Taiwan. Justice Rehnquist said this "should be left for resolution by the Executive and Legislative branches."

53. *Gilligan v. Morgan*, 413 U.S. 1 (1973).

54. Also see other cases dismissed as a political question: *South v. Peters*, 339 U.S. 276 (1950); *Matthews v. Handley*, 361 U.S. 127 (1959); *Radford v. Gary*, 352 U.S. 991 (1957); *Kidd v. McCanless*, 352 U.S. 920 (1956); *Anderson v. Jordon*, 3343 U.S. 912 (1952); *Remmey v. Smith*, 342 U.S. 916 (1952); and *Tedesco v. Bd. of Supervisors*, 339 U.S. 940 (1950).

55. The case concerned the procedures of the Senate to impeach Nixon. A committee was established to investigate and report its findings in a committee report to the full Senate. Judge Nixon would then be allowed to present statements on his behalf at such time. Nixon argued this denied his constitutional right to be tried by the full Senate.

56. *Walter Nixon v. United States*, 506 U.S. 224, 228 (1993). Also see Peter M. Shane, "Disappearing Democracy: How Bush v. Gore Undermined the Federal Right to Vote for Presidential Electors," *Florida State University Law Review* 29, no. 2 (Fall 2001): 535–585; and Robert J. Pushaw, Jr., "The Presidential Election Dispute, the Political Question Doctrine and the Fourteenth Amendment: A Reply to Professor Krent and Shane," *Florida State University Law Review* 29, no. 2 (Fall 2001): 602–623.

57. *Walter Nixon v. United States*, 506 U.S. 228, 230 (1993).

58. For more discussion see Robert Pushaw's analysis utilized in this section. See, Robert J. Pushaw, Jr., "The Presidential Election Dispute, the Political Question Doctrine and the Fourteenth Amendment: A Reply to Professor Krent and Shane," *Florida State University Law Review* 29, no. 2 (Fall 2001). See other works in the law review such as Harold Krent, "Judging Judging: The Problem of Second-Guessing State Judges' Interpretation of State Law in Bush v. Gore," *Florida State University Law Review* 29, no. 2 (Fall 2001); Peter Shane, "Disappearing Democracy: How Bush v. Gore Undermined the Federal Right to Vote for presidential Electors," *Florida State University Law Review* 29, no. 2 (Fall 2001); and Pamela Karlan, 'Unduly Partial: The Supreme Court and the Fourteenth Amendment in Bush v. Gore," *Florida State University Law Review* 29, no. 2 (Fall 2001).

59. Robert J. Pushaw, Jr., "The Presidential Election Dispute, the Political Question Doctrine and the Fourteenth Amendment: A Reply to Professor Krent and Shane," *Florida State University Law Review* 29, no. 2 (Fall 2001), 618.

60. *Bush v. Gore*, 531 U.S. 98, 129 (Souter, J., dissenting).

61. *Vander Jagt v. O'Neil*, 699 F. 2d 1166, 1178–79 (1983) (Bork, J., concurring).

62. For a general discussion on the relationship of the courts see: Edward Hartnett, "Why Is the Supreme Court of the United States Protecting State Judges from

Popular Democracy? *Texas Law Review* 75, no. 5 (1997): 907; and Mitchell Wendell, *Relations between the Federal and State Courts* (New York: Columbia University Press, 1949).

63. Russell R. Wheeler and Cynthia Harrison, *Creating the Federal Judicial System* (Washington, DC: Federal Judicial Center, 1989), 2. Also see generally Gordon S. Wood, *The Creation of the American Republic 1776–1787* (Chapel Hill: the University of North Carolina Press, 1969).

64. Section 25 of the Judiciary Act states in part: "That a final judgment or decree in any suit, in the highest court of law . . . where is drawn in question the validity of a treaty or statute of, or an authority exercised under . . . or where is drawn in question the construction of any clause of the constitution . . . may be re-examined, and reversed or affirmed in the Supreme Court of the United States."

65. See generally Maeva Marcus, ed., *Origins of the Federal Judiciary: Essays on the Judiciary Act of 1789* (New York: Oxford University Press, 1992).

66. See Federalist Paper No. 78 in Jacob E. Cooke, *The Federalist*, 521–530.

67. For a discussion on judicial review see works such as Edward Corwin, *Court Over Constitution: A Study of Judicial Review as an Instrument of Popular Government* (Gloucester, MA: Peter Smith, 1957); Wallace Mendelson, *The Constitution and The Supreme Court* (New York: Dodd, Mead & Company, 1970); Henry J. Abraham, *The Judicial Process* (New York: Oxford University Press, 1968); and Jack Knight and Lee Epstein, "On the Struggle for Judicial Supremacy," *Law and Society Review* 30, no. 1 (1996): 87–120.

68. Edward S. Corwin may have been the first person to use the phrase *judicial review* in the title of a 1910 *Michigan Law Review* article. On the origins of the phrase "judicial review," see Robert Lowry Clinton, *Marbury v. Madison and Judicial Review* (Lawrence: University Press of Kansas, 1989), 7.

69. For a contemporary discussion see Susan Burgess, *Contest for Constitutional Authority* (Lawrence: University Press of Kansas, 1992).

70. This landmark case established judicial review over acts of Congress.

71. The case established judicial review of decisions by state courts that involve a federal question.

72. The case is about the fact that despite the Eleventh Amendment the Court reviewed a case against the state of Virginia. The Court said the amendment prohibited individuals from bringing a case against the state, but not from appealing a suit initiated by the state.

73. The case is about the Supreme Court's review of the actions of the executive branch. The case concerned the government's confiscation of steel mills to end a labor dispute during the Korean War.

74. The case is about the Supreme Court's review of executive privilege challenges between the president and the special prosecutor investigating the Watergate incident.

75. In this case the Court rejected the congressional assignment of the comptroller general, who was acting on behalf of Congress to order the president to make specific budget cuts.

76. In this case the Supreme Court overturned the claim of executive privilege to wiretap alleged "domestic subversives without a warrant."

77. In this case the Court invalidated a legislative veto by Congress over the executive branch's activities.

78. For varied perspectives on the Court's exercise of judicial review see Raoul Berger, *Congress v. The Supreme Court* (Cambridge, MA: Harvard University Press, 1969); Charles Warren, *The Supreme Court in United States History*, vol. 1 (Boston: Little, Brown, 1926); Benjamin F. Wright, *The Growth of American Constitutional Law* (New York: Holt, Rinehart and Winston, 1942); and Robert G. McCloskey, *The American Supreme Court* (Chicago: University of Chicago Press, 1960).

79. See seminal works such as Raoul Berger, *Government by Judiciary* (Cambridge, MA: Harvard University Press, 1977); John Hart Ely, *Democracy and Distrust: A Theory of Judicial Review* (Cambridge, MA: Harvard University Press, 1980); Jesse Choper, *Judicial Review and the National Political Press: A Functional Reconsideration of the Role of the Supreme Court* (Chicago: University of Chicago Press, 1980); Alexander Bickel, *Least Dangerous Branch* (Indianapolis, IN: Bobbs-Merrill, 1962); Archibald Cox, *The Role of the Supreme Court in American Government* (London: Oxford University Press, 1976); Christopher Wolfe, *The Rise of Modern Judicial Review* (New York: Basic Books, 1986); Richard Neely, *How Courts Govern America* (New Haven, CT: Yale University Press, 1981); Richard Hodder-Williams, *The Politics of the U.S. Supreme Court* (London: George Allen & Unwin, 1980); John B. Gates and Charles A. Johnson, *The American Courts: A Critical Assessment* (Washington, DC: Congressional Quarterly, 1991); Henry Robert Glick, *Supreme Courts in State Politics* (New York: Basic Books, 1971); Arthur Selwyn Miller, *Toward Increased Judicial Activism: The Political Role of the Supreme Court* (Westport, CT: Greenwood Press, 1982); Charles Grove Haines, *The Role of the Supreme Court in American Government and Politics* (New York: Da Capo Press, 1973); and Michael J. Perry, *The Constitution and in the Courts: Law or Politics* (New York : Oxford University Press, 1994).

80. See generally Christopher Wolfe, *Judicial Activism: Bulwark of Freedom or Precarious Security?* (Pacific Grove, CA: Brooks/Cole, 1991); and William Lasser, *The Limits of Judicial Power* (Chapel Hill: University of North Carolina Press, 1988). For a discussion on judicial behavior see generally Jeffrey A. Segal and Harold J. Spaeth, *The Supreme Court and the Attitudinal Model Revisted* (New York: Cambridge University Press, 2002). Also see H.L.A. Hart, *The Concepts of Law* (New York: Oxford University Press, 1961); Glendon Schubert, *Quantitative Analysis of Judicial Behavior* (Glencoe, IL: Fess Press, 1959); Martin Shapiro, *Law and Politics in the Supreme Court* (New York: Free Press of Glencoe, 1964); John Schmidhauser, "Judicial Behavior and the Sectional Crisis of 1837–1860," *The Journal of Politics* 23, no. 4 (Nov., 1961): 615–640; John Schmidhauser, "Stare Decisis, Dissent, and the Background of the Justices of the Supreme Court of the United States," *University of Toronto Law Journal* XIV (1962): 194–212; Terri Jennings Peretti, *In Defense of a Political Court* (Princeton, NJ: Princeton University Press, 1999); Robert Carp, "The Voting Behavior of Judges Appointed by President Bush," *Judicature* 76 (1993): 298–302; and James J. Brudney, Sara Schiavoni, and Deborah Merritt, "Judicial Hostility Toward Labor Unions? Applying the Social Background Model to a Celebrated Concern," *Ohio State Law Journal* 60 (1999),1675–1771.

81 See Federalist Paper No. 78 in *The Federalist*, 529.

82. Ibid.

83. Ibid., 525.

84. See Federalist Paper No. 78 in *The Federalist*, 526. For modern works on the influences on judicial making, see Lee Epstein, Jeffrey A. Segal, Harold Spaeth, and Thomas Walker, *The Supreme Court Compendium: Data, Decisions & Developments*

(Washington, DC: Congressional Quarterly, 2001); and Lawrence Baum, *The Supreme Court* (Washington, DC: Congressional Quarterly Press, 2001). For classical works on the social background approach see Glendon Schubert, *Judicial Behavior: A Reader in Theory and Research* (Chicago: Rand McNally 1964); and John Schmidhauser, "Judicial Behavior and the Sectional Crisis of 1837–1860," *The Journal of Politics* 23, no. 4 (Nov. 1961): 615–640. See other works such as Henry Abraham, *Justices and Presidents: A Political History of Appointment to the Supreme Court*, 3rd ed. (New York: Oxford University Press, 1992); Sheldon Goldman, "Judicial Appointments and the Presidential Agenda," in *The Presidency in American Politics*, eds. Paul Brace, Christine Harrington, and Gary King (New York: New York University Press, 1989); and Laurence Tribe, *God Save This Honorable Court* (New York: Random House, 1985). Also see Lawrence Baum's extensive research. Lawrence Baum's: "Membership Change and Collective Voting Change in the United States Supreme Court," *Journal of Politics* 54, no. 1 (1992):18; "Measuring Policy Change in the U.S. Supreme Court," *American Political Science Review* 82, no. 3 (1988): 905–912; and *The Supreme Court* (Washington, DC: Congressional Quarterly Press, 2001): 155.

85. David A. Logan, "Judicial Federalism in the Court of History," 470.

86. The framers believed the judiciary would provide an "excellent barrier to the encroachments and oppressions of the representative body." See the Federalist Paper No. 78 in *The Federalist*, ed. Jacob E. Cooke (Middletown, CT: Wesleyan University Press, 1961), 522.

87. See Federalist Paper No. 78, in Jacob E. Cooke, *The Federalist*, 524.

88. Ibid.

89. David A. Logan, "Judicial Federalism in the Court of History," 470.

90. Ibid.

91. For classic work on the issue see *The Roosevelt Court: A Study in Judicial Politics and Values, 1937–1947* (New York: Macmillan, 1948); and Glendon Schubert, *The Judicial Mind: Attitudes and Ideologies of Supreme Court Justices 1946–1963* (Evanston, IL: Northwestern University Press, 1965). Modern political scientists have built on the work of Glendon Schubert. See David W. Rohde and Harold J. Spaeth, *Supreme Court Decision Making* (San Francisco: W.H. Freeman, 1976); and one of the most recent leading work in the field, Jeffrey A. Segal and Harold J. Spaeth, *The Supreme Court and the Attitudinal Model Revisited* (New York: Cambridge University Press, 2002).

92. These are the Supreme Court Justices that voted in favor of Bush in the case of *Bush v. Gore*. They are Justices Rehnquist, Scalia, O'Connor, Thomas, and Kennedy.

93. Richard Hasen, "Bush v. Gore and the Future of Equal Protection Law in Elections" *Florida State University Law Review* 29, no. 2 (Fall 2001), 390.

94. Howard Gilman, *The Votes that Counted: How the Court Decided the 2000 Presidential Election* (Chicago: University of Chicago Press, 2001), 174–176.

95. Alan Dershowitz, *Supreme Injustice*, 154–155.

96. See the work of Richard Lempert and Joseph Sanders, *An Invitation to Law and Social Science: Desert, Disputes, and Distribution* (New York: Longman, 1986), which extensively examines the judicial autonomy of justices and provides a framework for analyzing court decisions.

97. Ibid.

98. Alan Dershowitz, *Supreme Injustice*, 7.

99. The dissenting justices made the statement in their dissent on the application of the stay. See *Bush v. Gore*, 531 U.S. 1046 (2000).

100. See Alan Dershowitz, *Supreme Injustice: How the High Court Hijacked Election 2000* (New York: Oxford University Press, 2001); Jamin Raskin, *Overruling Democracy: The Supreme Court vs. The American People* (New York: Routledge, 2003); Lani Guinier, "And to the C Students: The Lessons of Bush v. Gore," in Ronald Dworkin, ed., *A Badly Flawed Election* (New York: The New Press, 2002); Howard Gillman, *The Votes that Counted: How the Court Decided the 2000 Presidential Election* (Chicago: University of Chicago Press, 2001); Evan Thomas and Michael Isikoff, "The Truth Behind the Pillars," *Newsweek*, December 25, 2000; and Pamela Karlan, "Unduly Partial: The Supreme Court and the Fourteenth Amendment in Bush v. Gore," *Florida State University Law Review* 29, no. 2 (Fall 2001).

101. See Peter M. Shane, "Disappearing Democracy: How Bush v. Gore Undermined the Federal Right to Vote for Presidential Electors," *Florida State University Law Review* 29, no. 2 (Fall 2001), 581–584. Also see Richard D. Friedman, "Trying to Make Peace with Bush v. Gore," *Florida State University Law Review* 29, no. 2 (Fall 2001), 818–820, 860. He argues the Twelfth Amendment grants Congress the authority to count the electoral votes and enacted statutory provisions in 3 U.S.C § 1–15 (1994) to determine electoral disputes. He also maintains Article II, Section 1, Clause 2 provides that "each State shall appoint [presidential electors] in such manner as the Legislature thereof may direct."

102. See *Bush v. Gore*, 531 U.S. at 153–158 (2000), Breyer dissenting. For more discussion see Robert J. Pushaw, Jr., "The Presidential Election Dispute, The Political Question Doctrine, and the Fourteenth Amendment: A Reply to Professors Krent and Shane," *Florida State University Law Review* 29 (2000): 613; and Richard Friedman, "Trying to make Peace with Bush v. Gore," *Florida State University Law Review* 29 (2000): 861–863.

103. Brief of *Amici Curiae* Florida Legislature at 24, *Bush v. Gore*, 531 U.S. 98 (2000).

104. Ibid.

105. *Bush v. Gore*, 155 (Breyer, J., dissenting).

106. Alan Dershowitz, *Supreme Injustice*, 7.

CHAPTER 7

1. See John Fund, *Stealing Elections* (San Francisco: Encounter Books), 2004.

2. E.J. Dionne, "When Did Voting Get so Intimidating?" *Washington Post*, October 31, 2004, B1.

3. See http://www.yesmagazine.org/article.asp?ID=424.

4. Elections activists have long proposed various election reform recommendations. For more recommendations that are consistent with those proposed in this section see the following: http://www.yesmagazine.org/article.asp?ID=424; http://www.archive.demos.org/pubs/EDR_-_Securing_the_Vote.pdf; and http://www.brennancenter.org/content/resource/lets_not_miss_the_chance_to_change_voting_laws/.

5. Steven Averett, "Touch Sensitive: Assessing the Usability of Electronic Voting," *Industrial Engineer*, October 1, 2004.

6. E.J. Dionne, "When Did Voting Get so Intimidating?" *Washington Post*, October 31, 2004, B1.

7. For further discussions see the following: http://www.brennan.3cdn.net/ce2b654a66ea2580d0_e5m6bh2yc.pdf; http://www.pennumbra.com/debates/debate.php?did=12; and http://www.projectvote.org/fileadmin/ProjectVote/Publications/Politics_of_Voter_Fraud_Final.pdf.

8. Michael Waldman, "Let's Not Miss the Chance to Change Voting Laws," *The Huffington Post*, July 10, 2007.

9. Barbara Y. Phillips, *How to Use Section 5 of the Voting Rights Act* 3d ed. (Washington, DC: Joint Center for Political Studies, 1983): 12–13; and Langlin McDonald, "The Quite Revolution in Minority Voting Rights," *Vanderbilt Law Review* 51 (Fall 1983): 1249–1297.

10. http://www.yesmagazine.org/article.asp?ID=424. Also see http://www.thenation.com/blogs/thebeat?pid=122699.

CHAPTER 8

1. Kenneth Janda, Jeffrey Berry, and Jerry Goldman, *The Challenge of Democracy* (Boston: Houghton Mifflin, 1999), 213.

2. *Reynolds v. Sims* 377 U.S. 544 (1964).

3. For a historical account of the intent of the Framers, see Alexander Keyssar, *The Right to Vote: the Contested History of Democracy in the United States* (New York: Basic Books, 2000).

4. See, for example, *Harper* v. *Virginia Bd. of Elections*, 383 U.S. 663, 665 (1966).

5. *Reynolds* v. *Sims*, 377 U.S. 533, 555 (1964).

6. *United States v. Mosley*, 238 U.S. 383, 386 (1915).

7. *United States v. Classic*, 313 U.S. 299, 315 (1941). Also see Anita Miller, ed, *What Went Wrong in Ohio: The Conyers Report on the 2004 Presidential Election*, (Chicago: Academy Chicago Publishers, 2005), p. 139.

8. *Reynolds v. Simms*, 377 U.S. 544 (1964).

9. *Black v. McGuffage*, 209 F. Supp.2d. 889, 899 (N.D. IL. 2002).

10. *Harper* v. *Virginia Bd. of Elections*, 383 U.S. 665 (1966).

11. Further examination of such cases sheds light on voting rights. In California, in *Common Cause v. Jones* the American Civil Rights Union (ACLU), the American Federation of Labor-Congress of Industrial Organizations (AFL-CIO), and other plaintiffs complained that some African Americans, Latinos, and Asians were disenfranchised because of the problems with the punch-card voting system in nine populous counties. District Judge Stephen Wilson ruled that California would have to replace its error-prone punch-card voting machines before the 2004 presidential election. In Florida, voters in fifteen Florida counties that used the punch-card voting system filed a class action lawsuit against Florida election officials, including Florida Secretary of State Katherine Harris and Florida Attorney General Butterworth. In *Coyner v. Harris*, they challenged the reliability of punch-card voting system and argued it violated the Equal Protection and Due Process Clauses of the Fourteenth Amendment. In Missouri, the Urban League, the ACLU, and the African American Bar Association filed suit in the Missouri 22nd Circuit Court on behalf of 250,000 registered voters in *Moore v. Board of Election Commissioners*.

The suit claimed the different voting systems denied voters the equal protection of the laws. In Illinois, there were three lawsuits. The first case involved minorities in Cook County and the ACLU that filed the class action lawsuit, *Black v. McGuffage* against the State Board of Elections and the Chicago Board of Election Commissioners. They challenged the election laws in Illinois that permitted election precincts using optical scanning voting machine to also use error notification systems but prohibited error notifications systems to be used in combination with the punch-card voting system. The plaintiffs maintained punch-card machines in predominantly black precincts violated the Equal Protection and Due Process Clauses of the Fourteenth Amendment and the Voting Rights Act. The second case in Illinois was *Democratic Party of Illinois v. Orr*. The claim is similar to the other case in Illinois except the focus was on county election. The plaintiffs argued the prohibition of error notification systems with punch-card voting systems violates the Equal Protection Clause and the Voting Rights Act. They asked the Court for a preliminary injunction to use error notification with punch-card systems in the county elections. A state court judge granted the plaintiffs request. The third case in Illinois was the *Wirth v. Election Systems and Software Inc.* The plaintiffs were registered voters who lived in counties that used the punch-card system. This suit was filed against the private companies that designed, manufactured, advertised, and marketed the voting system. The plaintiffs declared the punch-card system was inferior and the companies deliberately sold fraudulent products to counties nationwide. They maintained the companies violated the Equal Protection and Due Process Clauses because they were state actors performing a government function.

One of the few cases that was not victorious in using the Equal Protection Clause in an election dispute was the challenge of the California governor's recall election in 2003. The claim was not denied because it had an insufficient equal protection claim but because the court found there would be hardship on the citizens of California to grant relief. In *Southwest Voter Registration Education Project v. Kelly*, civil rights groups argued that voters in California were scheduled to go to the polls on October 7, 2003, to decide whether California Governor Gray Davis should be recalled and many precincts had not replaced the punch-card voting system. California's secretary of state insisted the state would comply with an earlier court order to update the voting system before the general election in 2004, but the October 2003 election had to continue as scheduled. The Southwest Voter Registration Education Project, Southern Christian Leadership Conference of Greater Los Angeles, National Association for the Advancement of Colored People, and the California State Conference of Branches filed the first suit in district court on August 7, 2003. They maintained the scheduled election's use of punch-card machines violated the Equal Protection Clause. They pointed out that voters in counties using punch-card machines had a significantly lower chance to have their votes counted than voters that used other voting technology. In addition, most counties that used the punch-card systems had predominately minority populations.

The Ninth Circuit Court said in its decision that like the district court that first reviewed the case it relied on *Bush v. Gore* as "the leading case on disputed elections" and considered the irreparable harm of each party and the public interest. It concluded the "hardships" fall on the citizens of California because time and money had been spent on preparing for the election. The court said the state began mailing absentee ballots twenty-nine days before the election and votes were being cast in the recall. It summarized, "The plaintiff will suffer no hardship that outweighs the stake of the State of California and its citizens in having this election go forward." Thus, the California governor's recall election proceeded as scheduled. Another case that was unsuccessful on the equal protection claim, but proved to be successful in showing a violation of the Voting Rights Act, was *Andrew v. Cox*. In Georgia, the ACLU filed suit on behalf of seven black voters against Governor Roy E. Barnes and Secretary of State Cathy Cox in *Andrews v. Cox*. They asked the Court to order a uniformed voting system because punch-card machines in predominately black precincts violate the Equal Protection and Due Process clauses of the Fourteenth Amendment, and Section 2 of the Voting Rights Act. The court ruled the claim violated the Voting Rights Act in which Congress in 1982 specified plaintiffs do not have to prove intentional discrimination, but did not violate the Equal Protection Clause without intentional discrimination.

12. The majority Justices were Chief Justice Rehnquist and Justices O'Connor, Scalia, Kennedy, and Thomas. Justices Stevens, Souter, Ginsburg, and Breyer each wrote a stirring dissent.

13. *Bush v, Gore*, 531 U.S. 98, 109 (2000).

14. Ibid., 108.

15. Ibid., 147.

16. Anita Miller, ed., *What Went Wrong in Ohio: The Conyers Report on the 2004 Presidential Election* (Chicago: Academy Chicago Publishers, 2005), 106.

17. *Daniels v. Williams*, 474 U.S. 327, 331 (1986). Also see a discussion on substantive and procedural due process in Pamela S. Karlan, "Unduly Partial: The Supreme Court and the Fourteenth Amendment in Bush v. Gore," *Florida State University Law Review* 29, no. 2 (Fall 2001), 588–589, 597.

18. *Duncan v. Poythress*, 657 F.2d 691 (1981); *Griffin v. Burns*, 570 F.2d 1065 (1978); *Marks v. Stinson*, 19 F.3d 873 (1994); *McKye v. State Election Bd. of State of Oklahoma*, 890 P.2d 954 (1995); *Bonas v. Town of N. Smithfield*, 265 F.3d 69 (2001); and *Siegel v. Lepore*, 234 F.3d 1163 (2000).

19. Peter Shane, "Disappearing Democracy," *Florida State University Law Review Review* 29, no. 2 (Fall 2001), 578.

20. Pamela S. Karlan, "Unduly Partial," 600.

21. Many legal analysts and scholars also discuss due process as an election safeguard for fairness in elections that are consistent with this chapter's examination. See one such analysis in Anita Miller, ed., *What Went Wrong in Ohio: The Conyers Report on the 2004 Presidential Election* (Chicago: Academy Chicago Publishers, 2005), 106.

22. *Miller v. County Comm'n* 539 S.E.2d 770, 776 (W.Va.2000).

23. Anita Miller, ed., *What Went Wrong in Ohio: The Conyers Report on the 2004 Presidential Election* (Chicago: Academy Chicago Publishers, 2005), 106–107. Also see Voting Rights Act of 1965 §11, 42 U.S.C.A. §1963i (2004).

24. *Mobile v. Bolden*, 446 U.S. 55 (1980).

25. Allan Lichtman, professor of history at American University, has testified at more than sixty federal voting rights cases, which includes several in the state of Florida.

26. U.S. Commission on Civil Rights, *Voting Irregularities in Florida During the 2000 Presidential Election* (Washington, DC: U.S. Government Printing Office, 2001), 11.

27. Ibid.

28. See Section 2 of the Act that provides in part: "A violation . . . of this section is established if, (a) . . . its members have less opportunity than other members of the electorate to participate in the political process and to elect representatives of their choice.

29. See Help America Vote Act of 2002, Public Law 107–252.

30. Civil Rights Act Section 245 of Title 18. See Anita Miller that makes this credible argument.

31. 42 U.S.C. §1973. Also see pertinent analysis in Anita Miller, ed., *What Went Wrong in Ohio: The Conyers Report on the 2004 Presidential Election* (Chicago: Academy Chicago Publishers, 2005).

32. Anita Miller, ed., *What Went Wrong in Ohio*, 107.

33. Ibid., 141.

34. See voter's bill of rights such as: http://www.ci.lexington.ma.us/TownClerk/Voters%20Bill%20of%20Rights.pdf; and http://www.heartlineweb.org/elections/PAGES/Voter'ss%20Rights.html.

Selected Bibliography

Alvarez, R. Michael, and Thad E. Hall, *Electronic Elections: The Perils and Promises of Digital Democracy* (Princeton, NJ: Princeton University Press, 2008).

Bott, Alexander J., *Handbook of United States Election Laws and Practices: Political Rights* (New York: Greenwood Press, 1990).

Campbell, Tracy, *Delivering the Vote: A History of Election Fraud, an American Political Tradition—1742–2004* (New York: Basic Books, 2005).

Dershowitz, Alan, *Supreme Injustice: How the High Court Hijacked Election 2000* (New York: Oxford University Press, 2001).

Dinkin, Robert J., *Election Day: A Documentary History* (Westport, CT: Greenwood Press, 2002).

Dionne, E. J., Jr., and William Kristol, *Bush v. Gore: The Court Cases and the Commentary* (Washington, DC: Brookings Institution Press, 2001).

Dover, E. D., *The Disputed Presidential Election of 2000: A History and Reference Guide* (Westport, CT: Greenwood Press, 2003).

Dworkin, Ronald, ed., *A Badly Flawed Election* (New York: New Press, 2002).

Ely, John Hart, *Democracy and Distrust: A Theory of Judicial Review* (Cambridge, MA: Harvard University Press, 1980).

Election Protection Coalition, "Shattering the Myth: An Initial Snapshot of Voter Disenfranchisement in the 2004 Elections" (December 2004): http://www.reformelections.org/research.asp?pubid=612.

Felchner, Morgan E., ed., *Voting in America*, 3 vols. (Westport, CT: Praeger, 2008).

Felknor, Bruce L., *Political Mischief: Smear, Sabotage, and Reform in U.S. Elections* (New York: Praeger, 1992).

Fife, Brian L, and Geralyn M. Miller, *Political Culture and Voting Systems in the United States: An Examination of the 2000 Presidential Election* (Westport, CT: Praeger, 2002).

Freeman, Steven, and Joel Bleifuss, *Was the 2004 Presidential Election Stolen?* (New York: Seven Stories Press, 2006).

Fund, John, *Stealing Elections* (San Francisco: Encounter Books, 2004).

Gillman, Howard, *The Votes that Counted: How the Court Decided the 2000 Presidential Election* (Chicago: University of Chicago Press, 2001).

Gumbel, Andrew, *Steal This Vote: Dirty Elections and the Rotten History of Democracy in America* (New York: Nation Books, 2005.

Harris, Beverly, *Black Box Voting: Ballot Tampering in the 21st Century* (High Point, NC: Plan Nine Publishing, 2002).

Herrnson, Paul S., et al., *Voting Technology: The Not-So-Simple Act of Casting a Ballot* (Washington, DC: Brooking Institution Press, 2007).

Jacobson, Arthur J., and Michel Rosenfeld, eds., *The Longest Night: Polemics and Perspectives on Election 2000* (Berkeley: University of California Press, 2002).

Janda, Kenneth, Jeffrey Berry, and Jerry Goldman, *The Challenge of Democracy* (Boston: Houghton Mifflin, 1999).

Keyssar, Alexander, *The Right to Vote: the Contested History of Democracy in the United States* (New York: Basic Books, 2000).

Lasser, William, *The Limits of Judicial Power* (Chapel Hill: University of North Carolina Press, 1988).

Miller, Arthur Selwyn, *Toward Increased Judicial Activism: the Political Role of the Supreme Court* (Westport, CT: Greenwood Press, 1982).

Miller, Mark Crispin, *Fooled Again: How the Right Stole the 2004 Election and Why They'll Steal the Next One, Too (Unless We Stop Them)* (New York: Basic Books, 2005).

Norden, Lawrence D., and Eric Lazarus, *The Machinery of Democracy: Protecting Elections in an Electronic World* (Chicago: Academy Chicago, 2007). [Based on the report of the Brennan Center Task Force on Voting Security.]

Raskin, Jamin, *Overruling Democracy: The Supreme Court vs. The American People* (New York: Routledge, 2003).

Rubin, Aviel, *Brave New Ballot* (New York: Morgan Books, 2006).

Saltman, Roy G., *The History and Politics of Voting Technology: In Quest of Integrity and Public Confidence* (New York: Palgrave Macmillan, 2006).

Thompson, Clive, "Can You Count on Voting Machines?," *New York Times Magazine*, January 6, 2008.

U.S. House of Representatives Judiciary Committee, *What Went Wrong in Ohio: The Conyers Report on the 2004 Presidential Election,* ed. by Anita Miller (Chicago: Academy Chicago Publishers, 2005). [Originally published by the U.S. Government Printing Office.]

Washington Post Political Staff, *Deadlock: The Inside Story of America's Closest Election* (New York: Public Affairs, 2001).

Index

About the Author

HERMA PERCY, Ph.D., is an associate professor at the Homeland Security and Criminal Justice Institute at Anne Arundel Community College in Arnold, Maryland, and a radio news director, anchor, and talk show host for 1430 WNAV-AM in Annapolis. She has had a wide-ranging career in politics, political science academia, media relations, public affairs, and journalism.